# LEADING
# ORGANIZATION
# DESIGN

# LEADING
# ORGANIZATION
# DESIGN

## How to Make Organization Design Decisions to Drive the Results You Want

## GREGORY KESLER
## AMY KATES

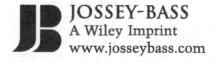

JOSSEY-BASS
A Wiley Imprint
www.josseybass.com

Published by Jossey-Bass
A Wiley Imprint
989 Market Street, San Francisco, CA 94103-1741—www.josseybass.com

Readers should be aware that Internet Web sites offered as citations and/or sources for
further information may have changed or disappeared between the time this was written
and when it is read.

Limit of Liability/Disclaimer of Warranty: While the publisher and author have used
their best efforts in preparing this book, they make no representations or warranties
with respect to the accuracy or completeness of the contents of this book and specifically
disclaim any implied warranties of merchantability or fitness for a particular purpose.
No warranty may be created or extended by sales representatives or written sales materials.
The advice and strategies contained herein may not be suitable for your situation. You
should consult with a professional where appropriate. Neither the publisher nor author
shall be liable for any loss of profit or any other commercial damages, including but not
limited to special, incidental, consequential, or other damages.

Jossey-Bass books and products are available through most bookstores. To contact
Jossey-Bass directly call our Customer Care Department within the U.S. at
800-956-7739, outside the U.S. at 317-572-3986, or fax 317-572-4002.

Jossey-Bass also publishes its books in a variety of electronic formats. Some content that
appears in print may not be available in electronic books.

*Library of Congress Cataloging-in-Publication Data*

Kesler, Gregory.
    Leading organization design : how to make organization design decisions to drive the
results you want / Gregory Kesler, Amy Kates.—1st ed.
        p. cm.
    Includes bibliographical references and index.
    ISBN 978-0-470-58959-5 (cloth); ISBN 978-0-470-91283-6 (ebk);
ISBN 978-0-470-91284-3 (ebk); ISBN 978-0-470-91285-0 (ebk)
    1. Organizational change.  2. Leadership.  I. Kates, Amy.  II. Title.
    HD58.8.K467 2010
    658.4'06—dc22
                                                                    2010034868

Printed in the United States of America
FIRST EDITION
*HB Printing*  10 9 8 7

# Contents

# Foreword

It was not long ago when "doing what comes naturally" was sufficient for designing organizations. Leaders were advised to simply hire the best people. Everyone knew that good people could make any organization work. Whether these views were valid or not, they are not going to work today. We are now in a different era.

The overly simple views of organizing have gone away along with the mass market. That mass market was served by mass production and reached through mass media. Companies sold stand-alone products—and each one was based on its unique analogue standard. When faced with complexity, these companies divided themselves into multiple divisions, each of which was a separate profit-and-loss center. They created corporate centers that allocated investment funds to divisions based on various portfolio models. Those models further classified the profitability and growth potential of the divisions into dogs, cows, or stars. The international business climate was characterized by deregulation and privatization. The best performers under this set of rules were companies like Hewlett-Packard (H-P) and 3M. Their organization design approach was based on the biological process of cell division. That is, when a business unit got to be too large, it was divided into two smaller divisions. And those two later became four, and so on. Each division was a fully functional and autonomous business. This model no longer works for H-P or 3M—or most other companies. H-P and 3M have gone outside for their last two CEOs as they attempt to transition to new models of organization.

This book, *Leading Organization Design* by Greg Kesler and Amy Kates, contains exactly the kind of advice that leaders need to navigate in today's business environment. Organization design requires the more thorough and more thoughtful approach that the authors demonstrate for us. Instead of serving a mass market with mass production, companies now face a fragmenting and segmented market that is served by mass customization. Instead of familiar Western markets, today's growth is in emerging markets with different cultures, active host governments, and state-owned enterprises acting as competitors, customers, and partners. Instead of stand-alone products and services, companies are being asked to integrate products, software, and services into solutions based on digital standards. Today everything can talk with everything else. Parts of companies that used to work separately now must work together.

So today leaders need to do what is required and not what comes naturally. The lessons that leaders learned—like "keep it simple" and "all you need is good people"—will not work anymore. What is required is the kind of explicit design process that Kesler and Kates present in this book. While growing up in the business, most leaders did not learn how to design and execute three- or four-dimensional matrix organizations. But by following the five-milestone process in the book, leaders can learn to design today's more complex and necessary organizations.

The book has some unique features that make it valuable. It is one of the few and certainly only recent books to take us through an explicit process to design modern organizations.

This is accomplished with the five-milestone process. The process is not a simple cookbook. Indeed, the authors have achieved a balance between process and content. They introduce the content at appropriate places in the design process. In so doing, the authors show us what to do as well as how to do it.

The other unique feature is the marriage of organization design with organizational change. Many of us believe that change begins with design. By following the Kates-Kesler process, companies can involve many key players in the design-change process. This is a good way for everyone to get his or her fingerprints on the design.

I recommend this book to all of the men and women who are charged with the stewardship of our institutions. The successful execution of leadership roles today requires an ability to design and change the organization. There is no more important and challenging task. *Leading Organization Design* should be one of the guidebooks for today's leaders.

*October 2010*                                               Jay Galbraith
*La Conversion, Switzerland*

# LEADING ORGANIZATION DESIGN

# Introduction

## Why Organization Design

A business leader can directly impact three levers of performance:

1. The *strategy*—where and how the firm competes, and where it chooses not to compete
2. The *talent* of the top team—the executive team that will build and direct the activities of the organization day-to-day
3. The shape of the *organization*—how power and resources are allocated to influence the decisions that are made and the work that is executed

Strategic decisions are first and fundamental. No amount of talent or organizational execution will overcome poor investment decisions. Talent and organization, however, equal strategy in importance. Strategy without a clear path to execution wastes the creative energy of the company's employees (Bossidy, Charan, and Burck, 2002).

The talent lever for strategy execution has garnered much research, writing, and attention over the past ten years. Although organization design and development have also grown as disciplines, there is often little connection made between talent and organization either in the academic or corporate arenas.

We have long believed that in order to reap the benefits of investments in talent, a company needs to create the organizational conditions in which all employees—from the front line to the CEO—can do their best work. In 2009, the Corporate Leadership Council launched a major research initiative to identify why so many leaders feel frustrated and unsuccessful despite the attention to selection and development of leadership in most companies. Its conclusion: "Leadership does not exist in isolation. Organizations must consider the organizational structure and macro and micro market situations in which leaders work. Strong leadership performance occurs when the right individuals and organization are available to address a given market situation" (2010, p. 11).

Good organization design enables effective business decisions to be made with a high degree of consistency. At the most basic level, aligned decision making (against a given strategy) is the test of an effective structure. It's logical to believe, then, that great talent is helped or hindered by the organization in which it is asked to work. Even though people will often find a way to work around barriers, who would choose that course?

## ORGANIZATION DESIGN IS A LEADERSHIP COMPETENCY

One of the most difficult challenges for new general managers who have been promoted after leading great teams in marketing, sales, or operations is to make their leadership impact scalable across an entire organization. Today's general managers understand the importance of organizational capabilities to compete, but many are less clear about how to create them. This book is about organizational leadership—aligning the components of the organization to execute strategy and removing barriers so that members of the organization can make the right decisions and do their best work. As strategies and organizations become more complex, it is not enough to be able to inspire individuals and lead teams. A working knowledge of organization design has become an essential personal competency for any successful leader today.

Among the many forces that increase organizational complexity are

- *Changing business models* and the need to manage a portfolio of varied business models
- *Innovation* in process as well as product
- *Global expansion* and the reality of competing with ever more sophisticated local players
- *Efficiency pressures* to increase volume, reach, and capability without adding overhead expense

Organizations will be as complex as the strategies and challenges they are designed to manage. But complexity, in itself, is not a bad thing. The ability to manage a complex organization that is capable of executing a complex strategy actually provides competitive advantage over firms whose management can only do one thing well. Today's IBM is able to keep many balls in the air at once through a complex web of structure, business process, and human relationships. It is a very difficult design to copy.

Heywood, Spungin, and Turnbull (2007) argue that it is important to differentiate complexity that is experienced by individuals inside the organization from the complexity inherent in the numbers of operating units, functions, and geographic units—the nodes in the network—that must be managed. Leaders sometimes make the mistake of trying to reduce the internal "experience of complexity" by reducing the product offering or by consolidating decision making. Although this may make the organization easier to manage, it can destroy value. Although the leader's goal should be to avoid unnecessary complexity, he or she must also avoid overly simplistic designs that don't reflect the level of complexity in the strategy. The leader should deliberately design the integration mechanisms and build the management team's ability to collaborate where needed. In this way, the organization can have as many nodes and dimensions as needed, while minimizing the experience of complexity for employees and customers.

When the multiple lines of reporting relationships in a company (such as markets, brands, customers, and geography, to name a few examples) are not designed purposefully, are out of alignment, or set up power imbalances, then the organization does create barriers to leadership impact and effectiveness. Establishing purposeful alignment is core work for today's leaders.

## WHY ANOTHER BOOK ON ORGANIZATION DESIGN?

This book is written for the business leader who wants to make better organization design decisions in order to execute complex strategies more effectively and to create the conditions for talent to succeed. It is also for human resource and organization development professionals who advise leaders on these decisions and who help guide the implementation process.

The most frequent request we get from business leaders goes something like this: "I know we need to change, and I have a fairly good idea about what I'd like to do. Give me a process that ensures I'm making the best decisions about the organization and that involves the right people. I want to be sure we're challenging ourselves to think creatively, but at the end of the day, I want the team to come together on a change that we can support and implement."

From internal HR and OD staff, we hear questions like this: "I'm often brought in late on decisions, or my client doesn't believe that using a process and involving anyone beyond the current executive team are even worthwhile. How can I add value earlier in the decision-making process and give my business leaders confidence in my ability to manage this work?"

With this book, our goal has been to create a thought guide for a leader and an executive team to use when making organization design decisions. Our framework for the book is what we call the *five milestone process* of organization design.

- Chapter One highlights the components of each milestone.

- Chapters Two through Fourteen present the models, concepts, and tools that we have found most useful at each phase. The chapters are grouped by milestone and are presented in a logical flow that generally mirrors how the topics arise in the design decision process. Each is also written, however, to serve as a stand-alone reference that can be turned to as design dilemmas arise.

- Chapters Fifteen and Sixteen look at organization design through a project management lens. We share a detailed guide to roles, involvement, and planning and executing design sessions, which ensures that the right people are involved in the decision-making process and that management time and other resources are managed efficiently. Chapter Seventeen specifically addresses leaders and makes the case for organization design as an essential personal leadership competency.

With this book, we are not attempting to be comprehensive. We make the assumption that you are familiar with the foundational concepts of organization design and come with some experience leading or working in organizations as they have gone through change. We imagine you, our reader, as a smart and successful businessperson or consultant looking for a clear and practical guide that will help you turn your accumulated experience into applied wisdom. Our intention is that this book will provide you with new thinking to add to your toolkit, as well as a coherent way to organize your existing knowledge about the field. In addition, we will share insights into how to make the organization design process straightforward and accessible so that it can become an embedded and replicable management capability.

## OUR POINT OF VIEW ON ORGANIZATION DESIGN

When we approach an organization design project, our thinking is guided by a number of beliefs that speak to both the content and the process of organization design work:

1. Good design always starts with a clear picture of the problem you want to solve. Structural change is often overly relied on or is misguided because the business problem is not well defined.

2. Organization structure is a powerful but blunt instrument for change. Changes in processes, people, rewards, and measures are nearly always critical complements to realignments in structure.

3. Organization design is both an art and a science. The best designs include smart, practical judgments rooted in a business case, supported by facts, and often developed through a series of hypotheses to be tested.

4. It is impossible to change culture directly. Culture is the result of decisions made regarding structure, processes, metrics, and talent. People are, for the most part, rational. When the environment changes, they will change their behavior.

5. A primary purpose of an organization is to make decisions. Decisions are influenced by power. Understanding power dynamics and how to shape them is essential to organization design.

6. Organizations should be designed with the expectation that great leaders will run them. Talent and organization work together to make a whole. Organization design work is not complete until the new structure has been staffed with the right leaders.

7. Organization design is an opportunity to grow leaders. Usually it is best not to organize around personalities, but often it does make sense to define roles that will stretch and grow great talent.

8. Organization change, like most systemic change, has more impact when leaders engage the right cross section of players in the design and the implementation process.

9. Having said that, design is a leadership responsibility—not a consensus activity. Design decision making should not be delegated.

The book shares our combined forty years of study, work, and learning about the field. It reflects the many sources of knowledge that we have integrated into our work and, of course, the clients we have had the privilege to assist. Four of the thought leaders who have influenced us and shaped our beliefs and approach should be mentioned specifically. Jay Galbraith is one of the founders of the field of organization design. The Star Model (Galbraith, 1995) serves as the foundation of all our work.

Walt Mahler's seminal thinking on leadership development and organization design informs our approach to talent and how to design organizations to develop leaders (Mahler, 1975; Mahler and Drotter, 1986). Bob Simons's levers-of-control model has inspired our thinking on the governance of complex organizations (Simons, 1995, 2005). We thank our friend and colleague Michael Shuster for suggesting the adaptation of the Simons model for this use. Finally, Dick Axelrod has taught us how to enrich the design process with multiple perspectives by engaging whole systems and large groups (Axelrod, 2002). We humbly share in this book what we have learned as we have built on the work of our mentors.

# The Five Milestones

ORGANIZATION DESIGN WORK NEEDS A ROAD MAP. Although the process is not strictly linear, we have found it useful to think about five steps that we call the *five milestone process* of organization design. Each design project will have its own unique path, with iterations and digressions from the flow that we present. There is no foolproof recipe that one can follow step-by-step to design the three-dimensional and invisible construct that is an organization. Organization design is both an art and a science.

That said, having worked across a range of industries, countries, and cultures, and for companies, government entities, and nonprofits of all sizes, we know that organizations can learn from each other and can use the same powerful frameworks to develop their own tailored solutions. We have refined a process that works in a variety of settings for units ranging from a few hundred to forty thousand employees and more. The process is quite scalable to be effective at the enterprise level or within business units and major functions.

FIGURE 1.1. *The Five Milestone Design Process*

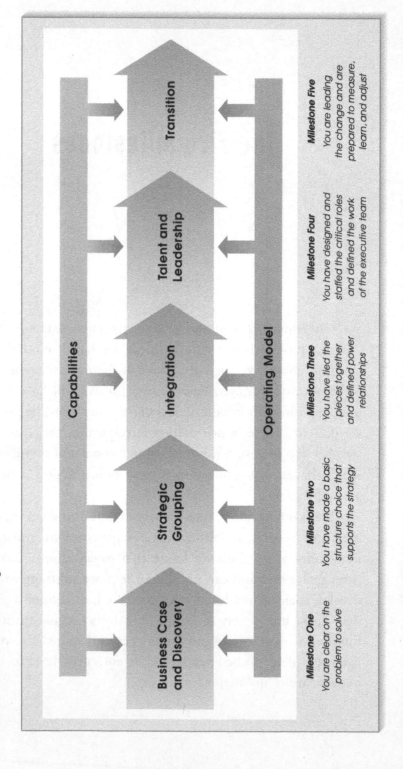

Capabilities

Business Case and Discovery → Strategic Grouping → Integration → Talent and Leadership → Transition

Operating Model

*Milestone One*
You are clear on the problem to solve

*Milestone Two*
You have made a basic structure choice that supports the strategy

*Milestone Three*
You have tied the pieces together and defined power relationships

*Milestone Four*
You have designed and staffed the critical roles and defined the work of the executive team

*Milestone Five*
You are leading the change and are prepared to measure, learn, and adjust

We use the word "milestones" deliberately to focus on outcomes rather than on activities. Milestones have been used since the Roman Empire as reference points along a road. They reassure travelers that the proper path is being followed and indicate either distance traveled or the remaining distance to a destination. In organization design, there are markers to indicate when one has finished a phase of decision making and is ready to move on to the next.

Figure 1.1 illustrates the five milestones model. The capabilities required by the strategy inform decisions regarding priorities and trade-offs at each milestone. Equally important is the operating model of the business—how closely related the parts of the organization are. The operating model affects the decisions made at each step by specifying how and to what degree the components need to be linked and integrated.

## MILESTONE ONE: BUSINESS CASE AND DISCOVERY

*Milestone: You are clear on the problem to solve*

The first step to effective organization design is to build a business case for change. The business case is made up of the key elements of the strategy, an analysis of the current state of organization, and a clearly defined set of design criteria.

Sound organization design decisions depend on a *clear* strategy, as organization design is a first step in turning strategic thought into action. Anyone involved in the design process must *understand* the strategy and its implications, and *agree* that achievement of the strategy will lead to superior results for that company. If the strategy is vague, full of conflicting objectives, or so broad that it does not set out clear choices, it will not lead to a workable organization. If the strategy has not been explained and understood fully, stakeholders coming into the design process will bring different assumptions that will lead to conflict rather than creativity. Finally, if those who must execute the strategy don't believe it will lead to a better future, then there will be little commitment to undertaking the hard work of organization change.

Once the highlights of the strategy are called out clearly, it is time to assess the current state and spell out the problem to be solved. The task is to assess the ability of the current structure to deliver the key elements of the strategy. This often means identifying gaps, but the organization problem is not always a gap. We work with many successful companies where the leadership of the organization defines a future change in the environment created by new technology, geographic expansion, or competitor moves, and initiates a proactive shift in strategy while the current business remains strong. The current structure is now misaligned to execute its new task. The "problem" in this case is to build new capabilities and create the organizational conditions that allow employees to do new work in new ways—likely with new behaviors.

Milestone One: Business Case and Discovery, contains three chapters to help you meet this first milestone.

### Clarify the Strategic Priorities

There are many ways to think about strategy. For our purposes, we need a tool that will allow us to test if the strategy is clear, understood, and agreed on, and to begin eliciting the organizational implications that will guide design decisions. The *strategy canvas* tool is a particularly useful way to educate a group about the organization's strategy and ensure that there is alignment on the major elements. We like it because the concept is quickly understood by a group, is easy to work with, and focuses on building future capabilities that differentiate an organization. The tool was developed by W. Chan Kim and Renee Mauborgne (2005) as part of their work on what they term *blue ocean strategy*, and we will show how to use this framework in organization design.

### Define the Case for Change

Once we are clear on the strategy, we need to determine what changes in organization will create new capabilities. To build a compelling case for change, it is critical to complete a current-state assessment that includes financial data, customer feedback, and analysis of the issues and opportunities, gathered through interviews and focus groups with leaders and employees in the organization. The six *design drivers*—management attention, leveraged resources and cost, coordination and integration, specialization, control and accountability, and learning and motivation—serve as a construct for analyzing the strengths and weaknesses of the current state against the business plan. The drivers also help identify options for change. They make it easier to call out the inherent trade-offs and tensions that exist in any organization design.

### Set the Design Criteria

To gain the most benefit from a change in organization, it is best to go beyond fixing today's problems and to think about capabilities needed twelve to thirty-six months into the future that will differentiate the business from its competitors. The capabilities become the design criteria against which we test all options. This practical and positive focus on creating strength is motivating and engaging for the design team and employees, and encourages expansive thinking that often results in more creative ideas than a problem-fixing approach allows.

Getting the design criteria right helps deliver better outcomes through all five milestones of the process. At every step, the design criteria inform decisions. They determine what basic units of organization will be most effective and what business processes, cross-functional teams, and forms of power allocation and governance will be required to bring the structure to life. The design criteria also inform role definition, staffing criteria, and the work of the new leadership team. Finally, during the transition step, the criteria are the way we measure progress. Are we establishing an organization that delivers the capabilities the business requires?

## Milestone Two: Strategic Grouping

*Milestone: You have a basic structure choice that supports the strategy*

Once the business case is spelled out, the next set of decisions in the design process defines the basic structure of the organization. Put another way, what basic grouping of work do we believe will best create the capabilities necessary to deliver the strategy? These decisions determine, in effect, the major blocks of work that will be managed by the top leaders in the new organization. Understanding the options for strategic grouping and the trade-offs among alternatives is essential to making good organization design decisions. Getting the strategic grouping aligned with the strategy makes the rest of the design task much easier.

Milestone Two: Strategic Grouping, contains three chapters to help you meet the second milestone.

### Use the Six Design Drivers

This chapter outlines the classic options for organizing on the basis of functions, geography, product, and customers. Selecting and blending the approaches to grouping create capability. The six design drivers serve as a practical way to assess the risks and benefits of alternative structures. The drivers are management attention, leveraged resources and cost, coordination and integration, specialization, control and accountability, and learning and motivation. Capabilities are often slippery constructs to convert into tangible actions for development. The six design drivers provide a logic bridge between a desired capability and the organization arrangements that support it.

### Choose the Best Grouping Option

Design is an iterative process and requires developing and testing hypotheses. Often choices appear equally valid—each with a set of advantages and drawbacks. A number of tests that draw on information developed in the Business Case and Discovery phase can be used to select from among the options. These considerations include the degree of change and disruption, primacy (what needs to change first), the management team's capacity to manage complexity, what changes will have the biggest positive impact, what will be most visible to customers or employees, and the fit with the existing culture.

### Embrace the Matrix

The matrix structure blends two or more of the classic design options into a single structure in order to gain the multiple benefits they offer. The matrix is unavoidable in most large multinationals today. It is often a necessary form of complexity, suited to executing complex objectives. Understanding the three basic forms of matrix can help when selecting one and anticipating the consequences. The first, at the simpler end of the spectrum and most common, has functions integrating across business units. The second type brings together front-end geographic or customer units (or both) together with back-end product or function units (or both). The third, and often the most complex for executive teams to manage, seeks to gain the benefits of global product lines or customer accounts together with the local responsiveness of geographic units.

## Milestone Three: Integration

*Milestone: You have tied the pieces together and defined power relationships*

Grouping work into structural blocks creates boundaries that must be breached to deliver a "whole result"—for customers, partners, and shareholders. If leaders are to make smart business decisions, they must define the power relationships among the pieces. Collaboration and coordination are expensive in terms of management time and attention. Thoughtful choices with clear, cross-boundary decision rights are essential.

The operating model for the enterprise informs each of the five milestones, but particularly integration. The operating model answers these questions:

- How much authority will be delegated to operating units rather than managed from the center?

- How independent should operating units be from each other? How much integration and coordination are needed among them in order to deliver the necessary capabilities?

- What role will support functions play in the business, and with how much power and influence?

As organizations become larger and multidimensional, decision making typically becomes more complex and slower. When accountability is shared, the organization can also become risk-averse and may suboptimize decisions for the sake of expedience. The goal of integration design is to allow managers and leaders to make better decisions without sacrificing speed.

Milestone Three: Integration, contains three chapters to help you design the most important points of linkage across boundaries.

### Design for Operating Governance

The holding company and the single-product company sit on two ends of the operating model continuum. The continuum characterizes the extent of integration needed among the units of a given company. Most large, multinational, multiproduct companies do not function at either extreme, but rather operate somewhere in between with portfolios of related businesses that have varied degrees of interdependence, shared infrastructure, and autonomy.

Although tension among these units is natural, many executive teams are not a robust enough forum to resolve the competing claims that surface in a multidimensional organization. We have built on Robert Simons's levers-of-control model (1995) to implement new tools for governing the matrix, including using shared beliefs, interactive networks, boundaries, and diagnostic measures to balance power relationships in a matrix.

### Allocate Power in the Matrix: A Case Study in Governance

This chapter presents a case study to illustrate how one company successfully used a variety of governance mechanisms to balance and shift power across the various dimensions of the matrix.

### Redesign Functions to Be Integrators

When the business is organized by some combination of product line, customer or market, and geography, the functions become a form of integrating mechanism at the corporate level and across the operating units. The classic staff functions—finance, IT, and HR—as well as business functions, such as marketing and supply chain, become the "glue" that links and leverages the organization. When well designed, these functions deliver the expertise and scale advantage that the large firm has over its smaller competitors.

Too many companies continue to struggle with unproductive conflict over power and role clarity between the operating units and the support functions. Without an integrating framework for designing these units, conflict arises over issues of centralization and decentralization. An effective framework aligns the design of the support functions with the corporate operating model to ensure that functions bring the right mix of oversight, linkage, thought leadership, and shared service support to the business.

## MILESTONE FOUR: TALENT AND LEADERSHIP

*Milestone: You have designed and staffed the critical roles and defined the work of the executive team*

Organization and talent are the complementary engines of strategy execution. A poorly designed organization undermines the efforts of hard-working people, who waste their effort on overcoming internal barriers rather than creating new products or serving customers. Conversely, an elegant organization won't substitute for poor leadership and missing competence.

Milestone Four: Talent and Leadership contains two chapters to help you meet this milestone.

### Design the Leadership Organization

Determining the number of positions and who will report to the leader in the new structure should be based on criteria that answer such questions as

- Where does the executive want and need to spend time, internally and externally? In what work can he or she add the most value?
- What is the extent and nature of dual reporting relationships that some team members may have to executives outside the unit?
- Where do jobs need to be positioned (vertically) in order to have necessary influence in the organization?
- Is the executive more comfortable with wide as opposed to narrow spans of control?
- What messages will be sent by placing given roles at the top versus lower in the structure?

Until the work of leaders in the new organization is defined, organization design is incomplete and unlikely to result in substantive change, especially when incumbents remain in the key positions. Executive roles should be spelled out in relationship to the business strategy and objectives that are driving the organization change. Leadership roles are also heavily influenced by the number of layers and the span of control that are embedded in the structure. Excess layers of hierarchy tend to result in narrower jobs with less freedom to act. As layers are removed, jobs should be widened with greater span of authority, with an eye to engaging high-potential leaders more fully.

Finally, not all leadership groups need to be teams, but nearly all need to interact effectively on some basis. The operating governance model of the business determines how closely the executives need to work together across the business units. When all the members have the same expectations about how often the group will come together and for what purpose, they will be more productive.

### Make the Right Talent Choices

Organization redesign opens a window of opportunity to bring more or different talent into the business. Building substantially new capabilities often entails making changes in talent. Leaders must act with wisdom as well as courage. We encourage a mind-set that ensures that the right people are in the right seats when the redesign is complete.

Capabilities and the design criteria, established by the first milestone, should inform staffing needs. Talent "pivot points" are those few and targeted skill sets that will have a disproportionate impact on results and achieving the business strategy. Like investments in new growth platforms, investments in new skills should not be allocated equally because not all skill sets have an equal impact on the capabilities you must create.

We counsel clients to avoid "designing around people" in the sense that design decisions should not be made to accommodate skill gaps in the existing organization. We do, however, design with talent in mind in order to ensure that roles are configured to provide the variety of experiences that will develop depth of competence and leadership. Many companies find that they are lacking a deep bench of well-rounded, general management talent that can move into executive roles. Organization design is an opportunity to design-in development positions; to create bigger, more challenging positions; and to establish experience paths among those jobs that can be used to grow future senior leaders.

## MILESTONE FIVE: TRANSITION

*Milestone: You are leading the change and are prepared to measure, learn, and adjust*

We have observed that after the intensity of decision making during the first four phases of the organization design process, the leader and the executive team are eager to get the organization back to work and to see the fruits of the design process. In their desire to refocus on the operating concerns of the business, momentum for the hard work of implementation can be lost. As a result, the full intent of the design is often not realized.

Milestone Five: Transition, contains two chapters that present the key learnings from our work in supporting the implementation of organization design.

### Set the Implementation Plan

The final set of design decisions requires leadership to determine how best to stage the implementation and the sequencing of tasks. The chosen approach is influenced by the fundamental reason for change. If the company is currently healthy but the design change is driven by an anticipated change in strategy, then evolution can work well. Evolving over time to the new state, rather than abruptly changing everything, is less unsettling to employees, allows time to build new capabilities, and creates an orderly transition from the current core business to the new sources of growth and profitability.

However, there are circumstances where a "pull the Band-Aid off fast" approach may be warranted. If the strategy choices are clear, and competitive pressures make it critical to move swiftly to recover market share or to stem financial losses, moving quickly can often make sense. A fast realignment often makes sense when an external change has already occurred and the current organization design actually hinders making the right strategy choices for the future.

Choosing the right implementation approach and creating a project plan to stage the process so as to ensure that capabilities are built in a logical way and account for interdependencies are essential for a smooth transition.

### *Navigate the Transition*

As soon as a basic transition plan is in place, leadership commitment to seeing it through becomes the defining factor in separating organization design changes that meet their objectives and those that fail because the new capabilities are never fully built. A full year of work, with significant leadership attention and involvement, is not unreasonable for a substantial reorganization.

Tipping points can be a useful tool to focus an executive team on the key points within the transition when a major step is needed. Tipping points in this context are tangible actions or decisions that are read by the organization as evidence that something very different is happening. Often they shift budget, authority, or decision rights from one unit to another; for example, global account leaders may be given veto rights in staffing of all sales roles in regions. Tipping points are symbolic actions because they have a disproportionate impact in altering power dynamics. In this way they are a powerful set of tools for executives to apply to guide, cajole, and course-correct their way through the transition plan.

## CHAPTER ONE SUMMARY: THE FIVE MILESTONES

Although organization design is not a strictly linear process, it is very useful to follow a set of process steps that are applicable to large and small design initiatives. The five milestones represent markers that allow designers to plan and manage the process flexibly but with a clear road map.

- Milestone One: Business Case and Discovery
  - Clarify the strategic priorities
  - Define the case for change
  - Set the design criteria

- Milestone Two: Strategic Grouping
  - Use the six design drivers
  - Choose the best grouping option
  - Embrace the matrix
- Milestone Three: Integration
  - Design for operating governance
  - Allocate power in the matrix
  - Redesign functions to be integrators
- Milestone Four: Talent and Leadership
  - Design the leadership organization
  - Make the right talent choices
- Milestone Five: Transition
  - Set the implementation plan
  - Navigate the transition

# MILESTONE
# ONE

## Business Case and Discovery

Business leaders have a strong bias toward action. By the time a situation has been tagged as an "organization design" project, most leaders have conducted their own analysis of the situation and formulated a number of options. We tend to trust our clients' instincts when they are accomplished leaders who have successfully faced many business and organizational challenges. They frequently do understand the complexity and depth of issues, and we often find that they are already contemplating a reasonable set of alternative actions. As often, however, we discover that the leader is heading down a path of solving the wrong problem. The intuitive diagnostic may be wrong. Or the leader may have a bias for or against a part of the organization she knows well. Or the leader may not have full access to information and be unaware of customer or frontline employee experiences.

Although one person can have a good idea, one person can't implement change. The process of organization design is nearly as important as the decisions themselves. The members of the extended management team who will need to support and carry out the changes have to go through the same discovery and design process as the leader. Each has to understand and be convinced that there is a problem to solve or an opportunity worth pursuing. Each has to explore all the alternatives and grapple with the trade-offs. Only then can each be fully committed to the change and lead others through it. Implementation is accelerated when change management begins right at the beginning of the project. When the employees in an organization are engaged in understanding the "why" and the rationale behind a new design, they are more likely to support the change.

Therefore, the first milestone is to be sure that the organization's leadership is clear on the problem to solve—that they have a clear business case for change and can articulate why the status quo is not an option. The three chapters in this part of the book discuss the tasks you need to perform to reach the first milestone:

- *Clarify the strategic priorities* and ensure that there is agreement and commitment to what will differentiate the organization from competitors
- *Define the case for change* through a current-state assessment and analysis using the design drivers framework
- *Set the design criteria* against which all design options will be evaluated

# Clarify the Strategic Priorities

ORGANIZATION DESIGN IS BOTH A TOP-DOWN AND BOTTOM-UP PROCESS. The top-down task starts with identifying the strategic requirements of the business and selecting a basic organizational architecture to support the strategy. Jay Galbraith's Star Model, shown in Figure 2.1, has been the gold standard for this approach since the early 1970s (Galbraith, 1995).

The Star Model has proven to be a simple yet powerful way to guide leaders as they align structures, processes, measures, and talent to support a strategy. The big idea behind the Star Model is that there is no one right configuration of resources. Different strategies require different organizational forms. Even within the same industry, companies with similar products and customer sets will need different organizations because each has a formula for success that requires different capabilities. That numerous academics and consultants have created variations on the Star Model over the past thirty years only attests to its status as the most influential model used in organization design.

The bottom-up view is focused on work and tasks and seeks to lay out business processes in an effective manner. In this

FIGURE 2.1. *The Star Model*

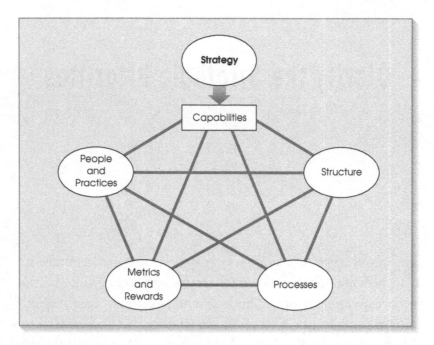

*Source:* Adapted from Galbraith, 1995

approach, roles are designed around natural work flows. Business process reengineering, six sigma quality projects, lean manufacturing, and work redesign are all techniques for rationalizing and streamlining work, handoffs, and approvals to ensure that work gets done efficiently.

Effective design marries the top-down and the bottom-up approaches. The strategic view determines the architecture and then design teams and function heads flesh out the detail below, tapping their deep understanding of the work, customers, and business processes. Design is often an iterative process, with both levels of thought informing one another.

The relationship between strategy and structure is less sequential and more interactive than ever before. Today's global economy requires executives to be more resourceful and to move more quickly. In this environment, it may not be possible in some industries to see clearly enough what is ahead to articulate three- or five-year detailed strategies for growth. Instead, business performance may be better served by creating greater organizational agility so as to enable maximum responsiveness to opportunities as they appear (Sull, 2009). Examples of this type of strategic agility include limiting the integration of certain acquired businesses in order to be able to exit sectors when necessary; minimizing the number of P&L centers in order to be able to make higher-level portfolio trade-off investment decisions; and developing cadres of international leadership talent that can be reallocated to new opportunities quickly.

That said, design needs to be anchored in some strategic priorities. Without a vision of a future state, it is too easy to make design decisions about roles and work flows that only fix today's problems. Organization design should be forward looking. Too often "reorganizations" and "restructurings" prescribe only the immediate set of changes, much like a shortsighted move on the chess board. A change is made to defend a position or seize an opening but without any picture of a larger, long-term strategy. To employees it can feel as if the organization is lurching forward randomly. They put their heads down and avoid fully engaging in the change, figuring that another seemingly arbitrary lurch in another direction will happen soon enough.

## Business Problems and Opportunities

Let's look at some examples of the kinds of business problems and opportunities today that trigger an organization design project.

### 1. A Significant Change in Strategy Has Occurred

The organization needs to change when the business wants to get something new accomplished—move into new markets, appeal to new customer groups, change the business model, or take advantage of a new technology.

*The Company Becomes Global.*   Many companies are still working through the implications of increasing global reach. As they come to rely increasingly on geographic expansion for growth, they need to create the capabilities to manage global brand architecture, develop and manage more multinational products, and leverage global assets (such as the supply chain).

*The Business Model Shifts.*   A business model defines the relationship between customers, economics, a value proposition, and necessary capabilities. Figure 2.2 shows an example.

---

FIGURE 2.2. *Illustration of a Typical Business Model*

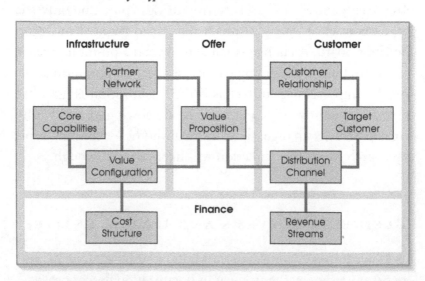

*Source:* Adapted from Osterwalder, 2009

An example of a shift is Apple's decision to enter the world of retail, which entails a set of capabilities different from its entirely wholesale-focused strategy, organization, and culture. Another example is the decision for Coca-Cola and Pepsi to buy back and integrate their operationally driven bottlers into their core businesses. Oracle is another company making a business model shift in the decision to purchase Sun and vertically integrate a computer hardware capability into its software business. Many technology businesses, large and small, have had to shift their business model from selling systems to selling professional services. IBM may be the master of these transformations. In each of these examples, new capabilities are needed, which require rethinking structure, process, skills, and measures.

### 2. Execution Gaps Increase Due to Outdated Organization Arrangements

When the business has a sound strategy and good talent but performance is lagging, then the organization may be creating obstacles to execution.

*Decisions Are Slow, Resources Are Poorly Allocated, and Role Confusion Is High.*   These are a sampling of common issues that get in the way of execution. They are symptoms that tend to become apparent in structures that have been shaped by time and events rather than by clear design criteria. They show up in organizations that once made sense but are no longer well suited to the task, and structures that have become overlayered and complex by trying to solve too many problems.

*The Company Can't Afford What It Has.*   Cost pressures are a reality in most businesses. Recessions bring new opportunities to face hard decisions with a degree of air cover from angry stakeholders. More leaders seem to be recognizing the shortsightedness of across-the-board cost cuts. The challenge is to reallocate resources to more productive work. This remains a difficult task, but the idea of strategic resourcing starts with being very clear about growth priorities and the capabilities necessary to exploit them.

*Acquisitions Must Be Integrated.*  Acquisitions and mergers are obvious opportunities to consider organization redesign. Some are deliberately integrated at the time the deal is done. In other companies, integration is often delayed, sometimes across a string of related acquisitions, until enough pain is felt in the form of product management gaps, fractured customer connections, and obvious redundancies.

### 3. A Change in the External Environment Demands a Response

A firm may have a sound strategy, good talent, and a well-designed organization, but if something changes in the environment, a response is required.

*Competitor Action.*  Competitors may expand aggressively into a geographic market with a whole new set of resources, such as a local product development and engineering center in India that can provide very fast customer support during and after the systems sales process.

*A Regulatory Shift.*  Health care providers, payers, and pharmaceutical manufacturers, as well as the many businesses that work with them in the United States, attempted during 2009 and 2010 to decode the future of the health insurance regulatory environment. These companies have generated numerous alternative scenarios that would require an organizational change.

*Gain in Customer Power.* When key customers set new expectations, the company often needs to build new capabilities, particularly if it sells business-to-business. Large global and regional customers are demanding global pricing, coordinated delivery times, and special handling of inventory. As customers create more internal coordination to leverage their size, they are forcing suppliers to establish higher-level management attention and new skill sets.

### 4. Structure Limits the Ability to Innovate

It is an axiom in organization design that structure follows strategy, a play on Mies van der Rohe's modernist architectural command that form follow function. In general, the organization should align to the strategy. But there are examples of organizational capabilities that create new strategic options. The Spanish fashion retailer Zara, now the largest in the world, defines the essence of its strategy as its supply chain capability. Design, sourcing, distribution, and retail are linked so closely that fresh product ideas are introduced in the middle of the season, to build on consumer trends in real time. One benchmark study showed that Zara only plans 30 percent of a seasonal product offering; the rest is a reaction to events in the market (Bain & Co., 2008).

Sometimes the organization needs to be designed to create new conversations that allow new strategies to emerge and be acted upon. This often happens in operationally efficient organizations that want to move beyond process innovation into product and business model innovation. They find they can't make the strategic shift because the organization is configured in such a way as to block the right conversations.

Baghai, Coley, and White (1999) argue that companies that sustain growth over decades do so by paying attention to three time horizons—ranging from short to long term—in very tangible ways:

- Horizon 1: Extend and defend core businesses
- Horizon 2: Build emerging businesses
- Horizon 3: Create new options for future businesses

In horizon 3, the idea is to create a pipeline—not just of new products but of new businesses, fully expecting that older businesses will stop growing or shrink (see Figure 2.3). The key to managing horizon 3 is to have real activities and investments, however small, such as research projects, test-market pilots, customer and other alliances, and innovation councils that launch, test, and evaluate options.

FIGURE 2.3. *Three Strategy Horizons*

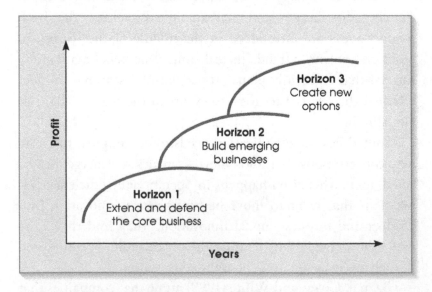

*Source:* Baghai, Coley, and White, 1999, p. 5

The implications for organization design are many. Some growth companies create new miniature businesses with full autonomy. Others create and adjust networks of people from across businesses as they learn. Still others spin out subsidiaries to create a network of partly owned companies. The skillful management of acquisitions is often part of this mix. In all cases, the company uses structure, process, metrics, and people not only to exploit the current business but to create the possibility of new businesses. Baghai and his colleagues argue that structure changes send signals about priorities and can be used to enable new options. Therefore, a continuous set of adjustments to refocus and repurpose resources allows the exploration of new strategies that wouldn't naturally emerge from the optimization of the core business.

### 5. A New Leader Arrives

In addition to these four situations, a common trigger for a design change is the arrival of a new leader. This is certainly appropriate if the new leader has been hired or promoted in order to address one of the aforementioned conditions. A thorough assessment of the current situation and some realignment are expected. Most leaders, however, are put in new positions as part of the normal course of succession. The incumbent is promoted, retires, or leaves to join a different company. The organization is fundamentally sound. The new leader, however, can feel two pressures. One is to configure the organization to look like his previous unit. In this way, he recreates the conditions of previous success and creates a familiar environment in which to work. This might entail changing structure, roles, or even bringing along some past allies. The second pressure is to demonstrate leadership action—to make an impact and impression on the organization, peers, or senior managers. Redesigning the organization is a highly visible and tangible action. This is the type of change that breeds skepticism and disengagement in the workforce. Organization design should be undertaken only when there is a compelling strategic reason.

## The Strategy Canvas—Calling Out the Strategic Priorities

Strategy defines opportunities and sets priorities among them. Effective strategy showcases possibilities, but it also sets boundaries and focus for management time and attention, and makes clear where resources are best deployed. Sound organization design decisions depend on this clarity. Anyone involved in the design process must understand the strategy and its implications, and agree that achievement of the strategy will lead to organizational success.

The *strategy canvas* tool is a particularly useful way to test if the strategy is clear, understood, and agreed on and to begin eliciting the organizational implications that will guide design decisions. We like it because the concept is quickly understood by a group, is easy to work with, and focuses on building future capabilities that differentiate an organization, not just on fixing what is not working at the moment (Kim and Mauborgne, 2005).

Most strategy discussions focus on finding success in established markets. Companies traditionally compete with product or service improvements that add more features or increase performance, or through price reductions in order to gain market share from rivals. Kim and Mauborgne call this the red ocean, using the metaphor of shark-infested waters made bloody by cutthroat competition. Blue ocean, by contrast, describes market space that has not been explored and contains new profit and growth opportunities. Although not every organization has a stated strategy of disruptive industry change or even of innovation, every organization must differentiate itself from its competitors in the marketplace. There are many ways to differentiate. Differentiation can be achieved through product or service features, quality, or price points. It can be achieved through geographic reach. An organization can also differentiate by focusing on one place along the value chain—for example, by providing outsourcing services. Conversely, it may be equally effective to offer the full value chain, in the way that many computer hardware companies are doing by buying software and service companies that give them an end-to-end offering and lock out competitors. Table 2.1 summarizes the difference between red ocean and blue ocean strategies.

Being clear about how the firm is competing and along what dimensions paves the way for organizational decisions. The strategy canvas plots the organization against a competitor or class of competitors. Along the horizontal axis are the elements of the offering. Along the vertical axis is a relative scale from low to high.

TABLE 2.1. *Red Ocean and Blue Ocean Strategies*

| Red Ocean | Blue Ocean |
| --- | --- |
| Competes in existing market | Creates uncontested new markets |
| Assumes that industry's structural conditions are fixed | Changes market boundaries and industry structure |
| Makes incremental improvements to existing offerings | Creates a leap in value for customer |
| Exploits existing demand | Creates and captures new demand |
| Aligns activities with either value or cost | Aligns activities in pursuit of differentiation and low cost |
| Focuses on strategy for the now | Focuses on strategy for the future |
| Beats the competition | Makes the competition irrelevant |

*Source:* Adapted from Kim and Mauborgne, 2005

High generally means more features and hence more resources devoted by the organization to delivering this component of the offer. In terms of price, high refers to high price. Figure 2.4 shows the strategy profile for Disney Cruise Lines in comparison to a major competitor, Royal Caribbean, in the early 2000s.

The strategy canvas shows that Disney charged a higher price and offered fewer itinerary options than Royal Caribbean. At the time, it was the only cruise line that offered an integrated theme park–cruise combination. Essentially, the cruise line was a brand extension that applied the Disney formula in a new context. By choosing not to compete with a variety of itineraries, Disney conserved resources and reduced the expense that comes with product variability. Resources were instead directed into preserving the brand through employee training and a unique

FIGURE 2.4. *Strategy Canvas for Disney Versus Royal Caribbean Cruise Lines in the Early 2000s*

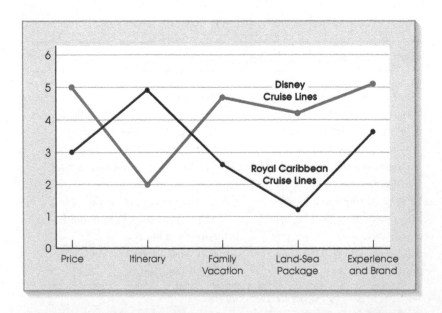

shipboard experience. Together with Disney's strong brand, family-oriented ship amenities, and storied service, the cruise line was a small but winning part of the Disney portfolio.

However, the waters in which Disney sailed soon became red. Royal Caribbean introduced more family-friendly programs and shipboard features, such as rock climbing walls and ice rinks, onto its ships. In 2009, Royal Caribbean teamed with Universal Studios in Disney's Orlando backyard to offer theme park–cruise packages. And although the Disney brand is unique, these product improvements on the part of Royal Caribbean, combined with more itinerary choices and a lower price, put the two cruise lines in head-to-head competition, as shown in Figure 2.5. In response, Disney soon announced that it had commissioned two ships to double its fleet and would begin sailings to Europe and Alaska.

FIGURE 2.5. *Current Strategy Canvas for Disney Versus Royal Caribbean Cruise Lines*

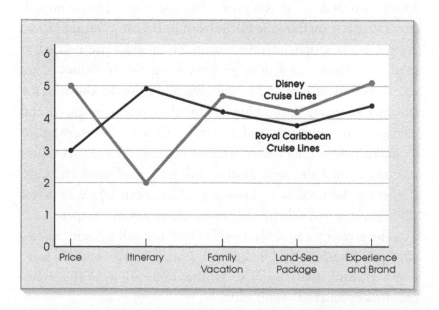

The strategy canvas highlights the strategic choices that have been made. The goal is not necessarily to close a gap but rather to compete on different capabilities than competitors. As Disney shifted its strategy to respond to Royal Caribbean, the strategy profiles began to look more similar. Disney will either have to find ways to cut costs (or margins) or create a new dimension of the offering that Royal Caribbean can't quickly match.

In addition, the goal is not simply to have the highest offering in the marketplace. A sound strategy makes clear choices. The strategy profile should indicate where explicit decisions have been made to simplify and hold down the cost structure, much as Disney initially did with its choice of a single itinerary. This allows resources to be invested in other capabilities that will differentiate, such as staff training.

The strategy canvas tool also quickly highlights some organizational implications of a strategic change. By diversifying from one itinerary off the coast of Florida to ports around the world, Disney adds a geographic dimension to the organization. Disney has to develop new pools of talent in new places, no longer able to rely on drawing talent from its base in central Florida. New processes that introduce more complexity are needed to plan, coordinate, and manage staff remotely. If Disney takes the direction of creating innovative additions to the offering in order to move into a blue ocean, then talent, research and development processes, and rewards will need to be realigned to make new product development possible. A more complex business model and organization will be forced upon the unit, triggering the need to make new choices about where to invest time, capital, and talent, and about where not to compete.

The strategy canvas is a useful tool for calling out the key strategic priorities and helping a leader and executive team begin to think analytically about the implications of the strategic choices for the organization.

# Define the Case for Change

ONCE THERE IS CLARITY AND ALIGNMENT REGARD-
ING where the organization is headed and how it will successfully differentiate itself from competitors, we can assess the
current state against the strategy and identify gaps and misalignments. Effective organization design starts with a sound
current-state assessment that includes review of the strategic
priorities, current organization documentation, customer feedback, and analysis of the issues and opportunities; these data are
gathered through interviews and focus groups with leaders and,
sometimes, with employees in the organization.

The assessment may be conducted by internal or external
consultants, or a combination of the two. External consultants
are able to ask questions that might appear naïve, uninformed,
or overly critical if they were asked by internal people. This is an
advantage for the outsider, who is learning the organization as
he or she goes, and who can build a baseline of understanding with
no assumptions going in. When it works it produces real insight
(even when the analysis articulates what everyone knows, but is
afraid to say).

The assessment should be balanced, taking into account the strengths in the current organization as well as potential weaknesses, relative to the strategic priorities that have been identified.

## WHY AN ASSESSMENT

It's tempting for the executive with a strong bias to action to skip or abbreviate this work. We will examine five reasons to do an assessment; we will also spell out the deliverables and what we have learned about conducting successful assessments.

### Define the Problem to Be Solved

It is simply imperative to clearly define the problem to be solved. Failure to do this leads to wasted effort and sometimes the wrong fix—which is often why multiple organization changes are often made with no change in business results.

A presenting problem is usually articulated by the top executive at the beginning of the discovery process. We listen closely to what executives have to say because they do capture frustrations and the obvious strains as well as aspirations for the future. But smart leaders don't want their internal or external consultants buying in to the presenting problem too quickly.

The full assessment will bring many complaints to the surface—some indicative of legitimate organizational issues, others more related to common gripes of working in a big company. Those that are rooted in deeper misalignments may be very important to evaluate, but without assuming cause and effect. For example, one of our clients had become frustrated with a marketing department that was widely viewed as ineffective. The leader had already decided, quietly, to replace the head of marketing. But the assessment brought important issues to light. First, a fractured and politicized reporting structure blocked any linkage between decisions made in the geographic units from those in the center. The heads of the geographic divisions revealed in confidential interviews that they saw no value in center-based marketing capability, beyond communications services, and they actively resisted a broader role for the incumbent marketing leader. The first problem to be solved was to understand the role of marketing in the business and to gain a degree of buy-in to that picture—in the context of a new design for the division. The effectiveness of the marketing head could be judged later, once the go-forward role was properly understood.

The current-state assessment must do more than report back what people in the organization are thinking. It must deliver a problem statement. This requires the consultants (internal or external) to articulate a fact-based, diagnostic point of view. An effective problem statement should be written in very specific, concise language that can be supported by the data. We often prepare a set of five to seven statements that capture the scope of the problem to be solved. Typically the problem statement is crafted through several iterations of dialogue with the key executives. This is time well spent. Exhibit 3.1 shows an example of a problem statement. The division president had defined the initial presenting problem as "We need to tie the front and back of the business together, get everyone on the same team; and we need to learn how to do integrated solutions selling and marketing." Note how the analysis evolved.

In this case, there was a bias on the part of the division president to critique the regional sales and service organizations and to underestimate the issues in the central offices as viewed from the regions. Once the assessment was written up,

> ## EXHIBIT 3.1. PROBLEM STATEMENT—INDUSTRIAL PRODUCTS CO.
>
> - There are major disconnects between the customer—represented today exclusively by the sales organizations—and center-led product, product development, and marketing.
> - New product development is widely regarded as the single greatest gap in capability today, leading to a commodity versus solutions view, lack of momentum in new products, and USA-centric deliverables.
> - Product management is distributed across functions (and geographic units) with fragmented and undisciplined roles and process (lacking a life-cycle view), low customer connectivity for the R&D organization, and poorly defined product specs for software development.
> - Marketing lacks effective role focus and vertical market specialization; alignment with the field is not strong, and processes do not bring the voice of the customer into product groups.
> - Sales teams' roles and skills need to transition from legacy-product sales to systems and solution selling. The current sales structure, sales role definitions, metrics, and rewards systems work against longer-cycle, systems selling.
> - Sales and service (front-end) organizational models and performance vary widely by region (and within regions) relative to vertical market specialization, key account coverage, and linkage between sales and service management.

he was quite objective in receiving the problem analysis and in working toward a comprehensive set of solutions for the business as a whole.

As we have seen, the case for change may be a gap, a response to a new opportunity, or an anticipated change in the external environment. An effective problem statement can be written for any one of these situations.

The problem statement focuses the next design steps. When design teams lose their bearings, which happens at times, they can reset their work process by asking, "What problem are we trying to solve?"

### Surface Good Ideas

An organization assessment not only defines the problem statement but also surfaces ideas and opportunities. People at all levels in the organization have ideas about what can be improved and where opportunities are being missed. Often those closest to customers, lower down in the hierarchy, experience firsthand the friction caused by organizational obstacles from which managers higher up are shielded. The assessment should be used to surface the latent ideas that previously may not have had any forum for expression. Often the interviews bring to light the seeds of big ideas that can later be developed. Sometimes there are seemingly obvious solutions that many people in the organization have tossed around for months. These should not be rejected or accepted, but explored objectively. They might be treated as hypotheses later in the process.

### Identify Resistance and Differences in Perspectives

The assessment identifies not just what issues of content to address but also the best course of action for engagement. Skilled organization effectiveness professionals know that the assessment is a powerful early element of change management strategy. Interviews with a leadership team may uncover that not everyone agrees on the issues or their causes. Certain groups may be more resistant to change, perhaps because they were targeted for downsizing in the past or perceive that they will be losers in any change, because of the style of the unit's leader, or because they constitute a local culture that has been isolated. Identifying these groups helps in planning the rest of the design process, including the engagement and communication plans.

It is important to engage people who are likely to resist. We have supported numerous design initiatives where the emergent problem statement makes it clear that one or more groups are likely to lose substantial power or resources in the future. It is best to bring these units, and the key influencers within them, into the design process early.

### Create Shared Understanding

People may talk with a few colleagues or a manager about their organizational concerns or ideas, but few organizations have a mechanism to identify a collective view. Employee opinion and engagement surveys tend to focus on job satisfaction or manager performance. Such surveys are not intended to identify organizational issues. The value of an assessment at the juncture of an organization design change is that it creates a way for everyone to become aware of what everyone else knows (Axelrod, 2002). Of course, different levels of detail of the assessment findings are shared with different audiences, but by receiving this information, people become part of a collective. They are no longer wondering if only they experience this issue. They feel heard and acknowledged. They see that their input will feed into the decision-making process. Once put to paper and shared back to the organization, the issues are no longer mysterious or so potent. Having a common understanding allows people to begin looking forward to solving issues. Without this, the current-state issues will continue to surface all through the organization design process, as employees at all levels feel the need to ensure that they are heard.

### Start the Change Management Process

The inclination of many leaders is to keep the organization design project small and contained. The fear is that opening it up to people outside a small inner circle will cause uncertainty, anxiety, and distraction from meeting current plans. There are few secrets in organizations, however, and rumors will soon start to circulate no matter how small the inner circle is kept.

The assessment can be used to start the change management process right at the beginning of the project. In addition to eliciting information, the assessment should be used to educate employees as to why a thoughtful process of generating and evaluating alternatives is being undertaken. Those who partake in the assessment—whether through interviews, focus groups, or surveys—should be given background on why the assessment is being done, what will be asked, and what will happen with the data collected. They should be encouraged to confer with colleagues in advance so that their input is not just a personal view, but instead represents their function or area. When leaders are open and transparent about the goals and steps in the project and the decision-making process, and employees know that in some way their views will be heard and incorporated, destructive rumors are reduced and distractions minimized.

## WHO SHOULD BE INCLUDED

The assessment participants should be selected on the basis of the issues and scope of the design. The strategic goals, financial and performance data, and customer feedback should inform the assessment. Interviews, focus groups, and surveys can all be used to collect the views of the employees in the unit or from partners or internal customers. We typically conduct one-on-one interviews with the leader, her direct reports, her key peers, and managers one or more levels down who sit in critical roles. Customers and the leaders' manager or board members are also sometimes interviewed. Focus groups can be used with mid-level managers and a sample of employees to obtain a representative slice of the business.

There is no fixed percentage that makes a good sample. The objective is action research, not pure research, but we're careful to stratify to avoid obvious categories of bias.

If the organization design trigger is a performance issue (the strategy is sound, but the organization is a barrier), we will tend to talk with a broader sample. In this case, the project is about realigning the current state, and in order to get to root causes, we need to be sure we are hearing what is getting in the way. If the potential change is likely to be met with political resistance, we may also widen participation to engage people early.

If the organization design trigger is a change in strategy that will require more significant shifts and new capabilities, we may gain what we need from a narrower sample. Employees lower in the organization will still need to be educated about the change and engaged in the process. They may be articulate about what is not working in the current organization. But if the new strategy makes the current organization irrelevant, then they may not be able to offer as much insight into what needs to be built to succeed in the future.

## ANALYZING THE DATA—THE SIX DESIGN DRIVERS

The first use of the assessment is to gain insight into the current state and to understand the gap relative to the desired future state. The second use is to stir up new design options.

The design drivers framework, which we adapted from the early work of Walt Mahler, is a useful way to analyze the data from the assessment in order to (1) articulate a set of future capabilities needed to execute the business plan, (2) identify strengths and weaknesses in the current organization design, and (3) begin to identify alternative designs.

Organization design is a matter of making trade-offs among various benefits. As an example, one gains the benefit of specialization from a functional structure, and accepts that there are likely to be disadvantages in terms of functional silos that might pose difficulties in creating an integrated customer solution. The design drivers help clarify the trade-offs embedded in the current structure as well as those likely to be found in future alternatives.

The six design drivers, shown in Figure 3.1, represent the set of generic benefits that specific design choices might provide. They are shown along oppositional spectrums to illustrate the inherent trade-offs and tensions that exist in any organization. Each is described in the sections that follow. The oppositional relationships that are demonstrated are tendencies only, and in a given situation, the dynamics may not exist in precisely the way the model suggests. In the design process it is impossible to achieve all the potential benefits simultaneously. Priorities must be set among them.

### *Management Attention*

This design driver takes the form of a structural element that forces management time and attention to critical imperatives. An organizational role might be elevated in the hierarchy to give it a stronger voice at the executive table, for example. Quality assurance, in a business seeking improved product reliability, is an example. Future growth activities, which might otherwise be

FIGURE 3.1. *The Six Design Drivers Model*

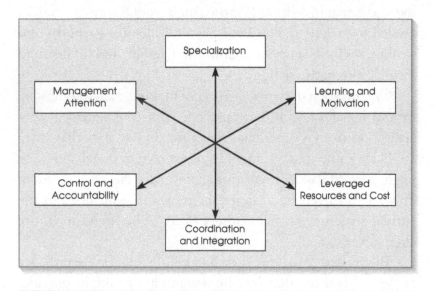

lost in the work of the core business, can be elevated and given disproportionate amounts of management attention. The unit may also be separated from the core in order for the leadership team to learn the business and in order to build new capabilities. For example, the country manager for China might sit on the executive team as a peer of the regional head for Europe, even though current revenue from that country is dwarfed by that of the European region. Another common situation occurs when an incubator for new product development is given the same organizational "weight" in decision making as the core product line. Management attention may also take the form of a functional czar for a process, such as strategic marketing or supply chain management, that has been weak or missing in the past.

Calling out and elevating a unit is often the most obvious solution to an organizational problem. It is appealing as a quick and tangible move. An executive is hired or promoted and given a clear role and set of accountabilities. The danger of overusing this driver is that the organization can become fragmented, and the leader can end up with a large, unwieldy direct report team. Executives in these roles often see themselves as accountable only to the leader for results, undermining teamwork across the leadership group. In addition, it can be an expensive fix, resulting in increased overhead as each elevated unit adds infrastructure, such as finance, HR, and IT support.

### Leveraged Resources and Cost

Leverage is used to create economies of scale by concentrating similar activities for maximum efficiency. Unless the organization is a true holding company, where there is no strategic reason to connect the operating units, corporations almost always have work that the operating units have in common, such as payroll processing, purchasing, or advertising. By bringing the work together and doing it in a standardized way, the firm can negotiate better contracts with vendors. In addition, because variation adds cost, consistent processes are cheaper to manage. For example, many companies have chosen to concentrate product development resources in order to deliver fewer, bigger bets into the market. Consolidating product creation may be a response to globalization. In many cases it is not effective or efficient for geographic units to continue to develop products exclusively for local markets.

Freeing up resources through consolidation has been a popular strategy. Leverage may take the form of an internal shared services center, or the work may be outsourced altogether. The concept of leverage is often used synonymously with centralization. However, if the design driver is to leverage resources to reduce cost or to concentrate scarce expertise, it does not mean that resources have to be centralized at the corporate level. For example, sales training can be done by one operating unit on behalf of the others. Or the work can be managed on a regional basis. Another option is to leave the work in the operating units, but agree to use common processes, platforms, and systems in order to be able to coordinate negotiations with vendors or to shift work from unit to unit as volumes dictate. IT organizations often do this with globally dispersed application development teams.

### Coordination and Integration

This driver delivers cross-boundary capability to the organization. It is a critical design driver when functions must work as one to build brands or satisfy challenging customer needs. All structures require some form of integration, but some must be specifically designed with integration as a primary driver. Coordination and integration often take the form of a specific role or a unit responsible for a whole outcome, end to end, cutting across businesses and geographic units. These units allow for another dimension of decision making laterally across the organization. Examples include product management roles, global category teams, and account or brand managers. Coordination and integration roles are a powerful way to link disparate parts of the organization.

To be successful, however, integration roles that bridge operating units must be staffed with players who have high credibility, strong influence skills, and the sponsorship of senior executives. Otherwise the agendas and priorities of the operating units can dominate decision making.

Other ways to coordinate and integrate are through processes, metrics, and reporting relationships. For example, shared metrics for the outcomes of a business process can align the priorities of units. When everyone has a stake in customer satisfaction measures, for example, the units that have an impact on customer satisfaction are more likely to work together to improve how the work gets done. Matrix reporting, colocation, and common information systems that allow access to common data sets all foster integration as well.

### Specialization

Specialization differentiates or separates out a role or group by expertise or functional activity. Specialization can be the right driver when the business plan requires real depth of expertise in particular areas, such as in technology or science-based businesses.

As the organization grows, it can benefit from scale. In the case of leverage, the goal is to reduce costs. With specialization, size brings the possibility of affording increased technical excellence. For example, a small company may be able to afford only a few generalist lawyers. As it grows it can afford to hire specialists. Centers of expertise are often used to bring specialists together. Examples are a central R&D function serving multiple product lines, or an executive compensation team in human resources. These centers build deep skills. Their competition is often external specialist firms. Centers of expertise need to combine their skills with deep knowledge of the organization and relationships in order to justify their expense. The challenge of specialist groups is to keep them connected to the business units—not just their internal customers but external clients and consumers as well. There is the danger that centers of expertise can sometimes focus on work that is professionally interesting and satisfying to the staff, rather than on what is important to the business units.

### Control and Accountability

This driver creates a single point of accountability and concentrates authority over a particular issue. Examples include executive P&L accountability for a product line, or country manager ownership of local government relations. Of course, designing-in accountability is fundamental for any role, but there are trade-offs here too.

Simplicity is the rule of thumb in achieving maximum control and accountability. Simplicity should be sought whenever it makes sense, but today's strategies are more complex, as is the external business environment. Sometimes simple solutions are not possible without walking away from key opportunities.

Toyota's response to the recall crisis in 2010 reflects a number of organizational breakdowns. Chief among them may be the murky lines of control for U.S. operations. During most of Toyota's expansion into America, the company's California-based sales division and its Kentucky-based manufacturing division reported back to Japan, independent of each other. Without a geographic executive in charge of the United States, there was no bridge between management in Japan and various U.S. constituencies—and the company found it very difficult to respond to the crisis with one voice (Holstein, 2010).

The key to balancing the benefits of accountability against those of other drivers is to clarify what results are most critical to control and to what extent they can be isolated to specific positions. As an example, profit and loss can be parsed into profit margin versus contribution, and roles can be designed to bring clear ownership to those component parts. Care must be taken to align the objectives of these separate job-holders to ensure that the overall result is delivered.

### Learning and Motivation

The final driver is an opportunity to provide leadership development experience and to empower teams to operate with high degrees of freedom. Although we are careful not to design around people and shape roles merely to accommodate individual interests, we do believe that organizations can and should be shaped to create development opportunities for the right talent. Jobs with smaller scope offer experience with less risk. Big jobs can provide challenges and allow the company to attract and retain high-level talent. Some companies adjust the size and complexity of regional general manager assignments in order to enhance development through lateral moves.

Organizations can be designed to motivate and develop people. Specialized units, described earlier, do this well for people with specialized skill sets: they build professional identity and credibility that have value beyond the confines of the company. Motivation comes in many forms. Often for technical and research staff, autonomy, state-of-the-art equipment and facilities, and challenging work can be motivating. For general managers, budget, decision making, size of revenue, and strategic scope are quite motivating. All organizations should be designed with the learning and motivation driver in mind. But here too there are trade-offs, often in control and accountability or in cost. Autonomy granted to product divisions often leads to high degrees of integration inside a given division, but may very well produce fractured results at the enterprise level. This can be quite detrimental to the overall results of the corporation.

The design drivers framework is summarized in Table 3.1.

## APPLYING THE DRIVERS IN ASSESSMENT

For each driver, we use the assessment findings to ask, "Where is this a strength today?" "Where is it perhaps overused?" and "Where is there opportunity to use this driver more?" The design drivers also serve as a framework for analysis that begins to guide options and choices in the next phases of design work.

---

TABLE 3.1. *Summary of the Six Design Drivers*

---

| | |
|---|---|
| Management attention | • Forces attention to critical imperatives<br>• Elevates an organizational component in the hierarchy<br>• *Examples*: Emerging-markets executive, incubators for new product development, functional "czar" for a new process |
| Leveraged resources and cost | • Creates economies of scale through the concentration of like activities (for cost management and efficiency)<br>• Includes centralized and center-led corporate activities<br>• Includes flat and lean structures<br>• *Example*: Shared service center |
| Coordination and integration | • Ties things together into a "whole" outcome, end-to-end<br>• Can be delivered through structural and nonstructural solutions—often process based<br>• Allows for another dimension of decision making laterally across the organization<br>• *Examples*: Product management team, global category team, brand management council |
| Specialization | • Differentiates or separates out a role or group by expertise or functional activity<br>• Ensures technical excellence—centers of expertise<br>• *Example*: Central R&D function serving multiple product lines |
| Control and accountability | • Is often an outcome of simplicity and clarity of reporting<br>• Elevates or centralizes problem issues to ensure that they are controlled<br>• *Examples*: Quality reporting to the top executive, product divisions with full accountability under a general manager |
| Learning and motivation | • Provides high degrees of authority and accountability on a relatively small scale, to allow risk-taking<br>• Provides diverse challenges, including exposure to international environments<br>• *Examples:* Small P&L units created to grow future general managers; rotational assignments, project roles |

---

Clearly the design drivers overlap at times. It is not terribly important that they be treated as perfectly discrete constructs. Internal and external consultants should become skilled at using them as a diagnostic filter. They are especially helpful in conducting an assessment discussion with line executives because they lend structure and discipline to conversations about what is working well and what is not working well in the current organization design, and begin to stimulate thinking about possibilities. Table 3.2 is an example of a high-level analysis using the six design drivers to assess the current state of a global product supply (GPS) organization.

TABLE 3.2. *Example of Current-State Assessment Using the Six Design Drivers*

| Design Drivers | Strengths | Weaknesses |
|---|---|---|
| Management attention | • Regional product supply director roles create one point of contact for group presidents, for all supply issues. | • Quality is not elevated sufficiently high in the global product supply (GPS) organization today—there is no leadership above the plant level.<br>• There is a lack of attention to an overall strategy for manufacturing and other parts of GPS. |
| Leveraged resources and cost | • There have been some early wins through the commodity procurement council. | • Decentralized plant ownership leads to higher infrastructure costs and reduced capacity utilization.<br>• Engineering resources are siloed in many plants, leading to poor allocation against priorities. |
| Coordination and integration | • Regional GPS director roles provide integration between product and commercial units. | • Decentralized plant ownership is a barrier to common standards, practices, process.<br>• Current regional GPS director roles may be too heavily relied on for integration with commercial units; they may act as bottlenecks. |

*(Continued)*

TABLE 3.2. (*Continued*)

| Design Drivers | Strengths | Weaknesses |
|---|---|---|
| Specialization | • Procurement has recently made good progress in building excellence in key material platforms.<br>• Local plants can be very responsive to local business needs. | • There are too many generalists in the GPS infrastructure to resolve commercial issues.<br>• There are major gaps in engineering support, especially for new products; resources are poorly allocated.<br>• There appears to be a lack of strategic sourcing expertise |
| Control and accountability | • General managers in developing markets continue to feel that they have direct control of local plants and distribution centers.<br>• High degree of local ownership for quality is reported. | • Subsidiary P&L units still own plant performance, creating conflicting priorities that suboptimize greater performance.<br>• There is some role confusion for quality results between corporate quality and GPS. |
| Learning and motivation | • Career development ladder from plant manager to subsidiary ops director to platform GPS director provides logical progression.<br>• Local ownership for plants is motivating—people feel like owners. | • With current governance model, it is difficult to export learning in all disciplines across locations—including quality.<br>• Individual plants demonstrate a somewhat isolated, inward view of manufacturing. |

# CHAPTER 4

# Set the Design Criteria

**C**APABILITIES ARE AN ESSENTIAL CONCEPT IN organization design. They are the link between the strategy and the organizational requirements that the strategy demands. Capabilities represent sources of competitive advantage. They are built through a well-considered blend of structure, process, talent, and reward systems (Kates and Galbraith, 2007) that is unique to the organization and difficult for others to easily copy. Capabilities serve as the design criteria for evaluating design options.

It is difficult to develop more than a handful of capabilities in any given company, so it is useful to think beyond fixing today's problems and to build organizational muscle that will be critical two, three, or more years out. In some companies, capabilities are an extension of the strategy process. Because they are forward looking and focused on building something new, they can be quite energizing as design criteria, and help to avoid a short-term, problem-solving approach.

Each organization will have its own short list of must-have capabilities. The following are some that are commonly sought by major companies:

- Build a brand
- Provide integrated solutions to global accounts
- Establish deep and wide distribution in emerging markets
- Build global categories
- Develop new products faster
- Manage strategic alliances and partnerships

What makes these capabilities sources of competitive advantage is that (1) they make it possible to execute strategy, and (2) they are difficult to copy. A group president, running the international sector of a large consumer packaged goods company, recently characterized the point this way:

> *The key thing that we're trying to do is exploit competitive advantage in emerging markets, but everyone else has the same idea. These markets are intensely competitive. So we must do three things: (1) deliver products designed for the unique wants and needs of emerging markets versus forcing those that fit developed markets at price points people won't pay for; (2) make them available widely and fast—in both the traditional trade outlets and in the modern trade—which puts a real strain on the supply chain (in India we have seven million retail outlets); and (3) do it at the lowest delivered cost, deep into the local channels. In India there are six hundred local brands that we compete with. They don't have to worry about any of the sustainability issues we do, and they have virtually no infrastructure costs.*

This is a very compelling case for thinking hard about the unique capabilities necessary to deliver results in these markets.

# AGILITY

We have already discussed the benefits of agility in some companies. As organizations get big, they tend to become slow and conservative in their decision making. Agility is a generic capability for many large, mature companies.

There are two general types of organizational agility. *Portfolio* agility is the ability to shift resources away from steady-state or declining areas into products, markets, or units that are likely to grow. *Operational* agility is the ability to quickly identify revenue-enhancing or cost-cutting opportunities (Sull, 2009).

Organizational choices may be quite different for portfolio agility than they would be for operational agility. The Star Model can be used to highlight the different arrangements likely to drive the two different kinds of agility. For portfolio agility, you are more likely to see organization designs that are centralized with robust portfolio management processes and a focus on return-on-assets measures. Companies that seek operational agility are more likely to operate in more decentralized structures and governance; focus on such core business processes as innovation, supply chain, and customer management; and use metrics to closely track operating and customer trends (see Table 4.1).

# EXTERNAL BENCHMARKING

Benchmarking can be valuable in design work, but should be used with caution. Other companies in the same industry often struggle with the same issues and haven't necessarily solved them. A competitor's successes may not represent best practices because they are achieved in a company that is at a different stage in its life cycle and competing on a different set of capabilities. However, analyzing other organizations and the

TABLE 4.1. *Comparison of Design Features for Each "Star Point" Likely to Support Portfolio Versus Operational Agility Capabilities*

|  | Portfolio Agility | Operational Agility |
|---|---|---|
| **Structure** | Power in the center facilitates movement of resources and investments | Power distributed into business units to ensure flexible response to market and operational opportunities |
| **Process** | Emphasis on portfolio management across business units; high visibility to all businesses | Emphasis on innovation, supply chain, customer management, and other core business processes |
| **Metrics** | Clear, few priorities managed at the top; ROA focus to guide investment decisions; insights into life cycle | Strong customer and market data, robust revenue and profitability data, lean and black-belt metrics |
| **People** | Common talent identification and promotion processes, facilitating the movement of people across boundaries | Cross-business and cross-functional experiences, outside talent, exposure to new ideas, higher-risk profile in leaders |

choices they have made can stimulate possibilities and may yield some learning. To stretch the design team's thinking, it's often useful to look outside the industry to find examples of successful firms that have already built similar capabilities.

For example, perhaps the organization wants to become better at getting new products quickly to market. Regardless of the industry, it might be worth looking at how Reckitt Benckiser, the U.K.-based producer of Lysol, Airwick, and Clearasil, manages its new product development process. Although it is dwarfed by P&G and Unilever, Reckitt is tremendously successful in developing not only new product features but also delivery mechanisms. Product innovations include hands-free soap for the home, motion-triggered air fresheners, and a tube for dispensing cough drops (Sonne, 2010). Reckitt has mastered the capability of open R&D using the IdeaLink Web site to post problems to which external scientists and technicians can respond. As a result, in the 2000s, 35 to 40 percent of sales came from innovations introduced in the past three years.

## How to Set Capabilities as Design Criteria

One does not move on to the next milestone without a set of criteria against which to judge future design options. Once the business strategy has been clarified and the current organization has been evaluated, it is time to set criteria for a future design. A well-articulated set of organizational capabilities—a concrete definition of what the organization must do very well to execute its plans—is often an effective set of design criteria.

This step cannot be reduced to a formula. Typically we work with the business strategy highlights and an assessed problem statement to articulate a draft list of future capabilities. These will be reviewed with senior leaders, and successive drafts will lead to a well-defined set of design criteria. The key is to make certain that a range of design options can be tested against the criteria. The criteria must be specific enough to be observable in the design options, and they must be comprehensive enough collectively to represent the strategic organizational needs of the business. In order for capabilities to serve as design criteria, they must be quite specific to the needs of a given business. In addition, they should be measureable, as these become the leading indicators against which implementation progress will be measured. Table 4.2 is an example of how generic capabilities are expressed as specific design criteria for a global company that creates and sells business optimization software.

The assessment plays a key role in isolating a set of design criteria like those in the example. Capabilities can be

TABLE 4.2. *Capabilities Stated as Design Criteria*

| General Capability | Design Criteria Specific to the Organization |
| --- | --- |
| Global marketing excellence | Customer-dedicated, center-led marketing (with regional presence) with strong voice-of-customer in information systems markets |
| Product management effectiveness | Effective life-cycle management of distinct portfolios of solutions that profitably meet diverging customer needs |
| New integrated solutions development | Speed-to-market and customer focus in new product introductions, including building scale in software development and support |
| Team selling for integrated solutions | Selling systems solutions into senior management levels, supported by product, finance, and technical depth |
| Professional services delivery and support | A competitive and profitable service offering as part of an integrated solution |
| Key and global account management | Clear sales ownership and skill alignment for key and global accounts |

a slippery construct. It is easy to brainstorm long lists of them, related to any given strategy. A capability like "flexible supply chain" may need to be pressure tested before it is used as an organization design criterion. Diagnostic assessment work helps winnow the wish list down and give the criteria more tangible quality.

In assessment interviews, problems tend to be the focus of energy. Critical incidents like lost accounts, failed product launches, and internal competition among operating units can be very instructive. We have seen how the six design drivers force a comprehensive, disciplined interpretation of the raw data, with an understanding of the trade-offs. We can ask the question in the assessment process: "What is more important to executing this strategy: faster response time (through an integrated business unit at the local level) or greater leverage (that comes from a more functional approach)?"

A series of assessment interviews will produce a great deal of "negative" information, even with the most balanced approach to questioning. The process of boiling the themes down to the most critical issues is in itself a calibration exercise. Which of these problems most need to be solved in order to deliver on the strategy? By asking, "If this problem were to be solved, what would we see happening?"we can turn a handful of key problem statements into future-oriented, positive statements that serve as design criteria.

Let's take an example: a problem statement indicates that poor connectivity between new product development teams and the supply chain organization must be given high priority in terms of its importance to the business, relative to all the other opportunities for improvement. In terms of the six design drivers, how critical is integration of supply chain resources with the product teams as opposed to the leverage that a centralized supply chain organization creates? These concrete issues pull us out of the conceptual world quickly. Debating the trade-offs is a titration process, concentrating management focus on the most critical. But to keep the process focused on the future, it's important to tie the debate to the strategy and capability, rather than allow it to be drawn toward urgent pinch points. In the example given, we may decide that we are willing to trade some efficiency in order to link fast supply chain decision making into the new product commercialization process. In so doing we have created a design criterion we might summarize as "close linkage of product sourcing into the new product commercialization process." This is much more specific than "flexible supply chain" and much more useful from a design point of view. How this criterion is achieved remains an open question. It may require a structural fix, or it may be achieved through a process or other integrator. That is not our concern at this point.

How specific the design criteria need to be depends on the level of organization that is being designed. In a systemwide design, a set of broad capabilities may guide organization design. Then within business units and functions, design criteria will become more specific and will likely be informed by detailed issues and problems revealed in the assessment process.

A clear set of design criteria makes it possible to now begin identifying design options. The criteria will be used in the Strategic Grouping phase to evaluate high-level structure alternatives, and later they will be used to seek ways to link those structural groups back together in the Integration phase. Often they are adjusted in later stages of the design work as leaders become more informed about the task, but compromises in the criteria should be taken carefully throughout the design process. Eventually the team should judge the effectiveness of its work against these criteria.

# Milestone One Summary: Business Case and Discovery

*Chapter Two: Clarify the Strategic Priorities*

- Organization design should start with a top-down view based on the requirements of the business strategy. A bottom-up view can then follow, which takes into account work design and business process changes that should be blended with the top-down view at the appropriate time.

- Key highlights and priorities from the strategic plan serve as the anchor for the major design decisions.

- Organization designers should know when a design change is likely to be an effective solution. Those circumstances include

  - A change in strategy

  - Execution gaps

  - Changes in the external environment

- The need to force a new dialogue with a new set of players to find growth opportunities

- A change in leadership (sometimes)

- To pave the way to organization decisions, it is useful to work with one or more strategy models that help call out how the business has chosen to compete in its markets.

- Dialogue and diagnostic thinking, focused on organization design, can help the leadership team align around the strategy.

*Chapter Three: Define the Case for Change*

- It is critical to be clear about what problem you intend to solve. The lack of a clear problem statement leads to scope creep, delays, and poor design decisions.

- Assessment is the process of identifying strengths and weaknesses in the current organization configuration. Gathering data and building a robust diagnosis should be performed in order to

  - Define the problem effectively

  - Surface good ideas for future design

  - Identify resistance and differences in perspectives

  - Create shared understanding of the issues

  - Start the change management process

- Be purposeful about selecting who will participate in the assessment, with attention to the scope and nature of the problem. A broad base of early involvement is usually beneficial to the change process later on.

- The six design drivers serve as a lens to examine assessment data and interpret findings. The six design drivers are

  - Management attention

  - Leveraged resources and cost

- Coordination and integration
- Specialization
- Control and accountability
- Learning and motivation

*Chapter Four: Set the Design Criteria*

- Design criteria should be set based on the business plan and the assessment findings. They are the means to evaluate potential design options.

- Organizational capabilities are powerful design criteria. They spell out what the organization must be very effective at doing in order to execute its strategies.

- The set of capabilities selected to serve as design criteria need to be crafted into a relatively short list of items that are quite specific and that taken together represent the capabilities most critical to the business.

# MILESTONE
# TWO

## Strategic Grouping

MILESTONE: YOU HAVE MADE
A BASIC STRUCTURE CHOICE THAT
SUPPORTS THE STRATEGY

More than thirty-five years ago, Peter Drucker challenged executives to think about the "building blocks and basic materials" of organization (1973). Expanding on the architectural metaphor, he encouraged leaders to identify the "major load-bearing units" of structure. *Strategic grouping* is the task of identifying these basic organizational units, which set in place the core power and decision-making relationships in the company. Once a clear business case has been defined, strategic grouping is the first set of decisions made in the design process.

Changes to structure are often confused with simplistic movements of reporting relationships on an organization chart. Rightfully, organization designers are quick to learn that a focus on structure and reporting relationships alone does not offer a complete view of the organization. However, overlooking the impact that structure has on the effectiveness of an organization is an equally large mistake.

We prefer the term *strategic grouping* to describe the first set of design choices. The term reinforces the top-down, strategy-led nature of the task. Structural options are a part of the strategic grouping decision, but not the whole of it. In strategic grouping we are seeking to understand the ways in which we can group work, power, and authority to build specific capabilities. In this section we

- Review the building blocks of design—the basic structures that represent the primary logics around which to configure the organization—and apply the design drivers framework as a way to analyze options for building specific capabilities
- Present frameworks for selecting the best strategic grouping option for specific organizational situations
- Consider how to configure common forms of the matrix to achieve multiple capabilities

# Use the Six Design Drivers

STRATEGIC GROUPING BEGINS WITH BREAKING tasks apart and grouping them into logical clusters. This work needs to be done whether the focus is on the entire enterprise or a business unit or function located a number of layers down in the organization. Strategic grouping requires the unit's leader to take a big-picture view of the work necessary to execute the business plan—a top-down view. Put another way, strategic grouping answers the question, "What basic grouping of work do we believe will best create the capabilities necessary to deliver the strategy?" Later, a bottom-up view will define the business and management processes that are also required to ensure capability development. But first, much like engineers creating the basic architecture, organization designers identify the major load-bearing units that must carry the business forward.

## THE BUILDING BLOCKS

The options for strategic grouping are limited, as there are only so many ways you can assign ownership for work. There are four basic building blocks (Kates and Galbraith, 2007):

1. Function, or know-how
   - A functional structure is organized around major activity groups, such as finance, human resources, research and development, manufacturing, and marketing. All employees in each function are managed together in order to promote sharing of knowledge, depth of expertise, and specialization. Functional structures can promote standardization and reduce duplication, and create economies of scale.

2. Geography or region
   - The geographic dimension is employed as a company saturates its home market and grows by expanding into new territories. When culture, language, or political factors influence buying patterns, or when consumer behavior differs significantly by region, a geographic structure provides the local focus that can create competitive advantage. The benefit of having local managers focused on these differences is that they can tailor the company's standard products for local tastes and compete successfully against companies that are more familiar with the local market. A geographic structure is also useful when the cost of transporting products is high, or when a service must be delivered locally.

3. Product
   - Typically, a functional structure evolves into a product structure when a company finds itself with multiple product lines that diverge in their underlying business models.

These new product lines require different organizational capabilities and a different configuration of functional expertise. Therefore, the companies will likely set up a new product division for each business. The launch of a product line that requires its own organizational home will often result in a new profit center as well; therefore, the terms *product division* and *business unit* are often used interchangeably.

4. Customer or market
   • Functional, product, and geographic structures offer benefits for managers, but they do not necessarily provide an easy interface for the customer. Customers, particularly businesses buying from one another, often want a single point of contact, products customized to meet their needs, or an integrated bundle of services and products. The customer structure looks much like the product structure, except that divisions are based on customer segments, which are groups of customers that share similar needs, characteristics, or buying patterns. Such a structure allows for a dedicated service relationship. Categories are another form of customer alignment. Categories and brands can be easily confused with products, but are more accurately regarded as consumer-focused market segments.

Table 5.1 summarizes the general advantages and disadvantages of these building block structures.

## THE SIX DESIGN DRIVERS

Each of the basic building block options for strategic grouping brings a set of benefits and drawbacks, as described in Table 5.1. Such generic pros and cons, however, are not the

TABLE 5.1. *Advantages and Disadvantages of the Classic Design Options*

| Option | Advantages | Disadvantages |
|---|---|---|
| **1. Function**<br>*Organized around major activity groups, such as research and development, operations, marketing, finance, and human resources* | Delivers increased knowledge sharing within functions and ability to build depth and specialization. Attracts and develops experts who "speak the same language"<br>Creates leverage with vendors<br>Produces economies of scale and standardization of processes and procedures | Can make it difficult to manage diverse product and service lines<br>Leads to contention among cross-functional processes<br>May lead to conflicting priorities that do not capture customer needs<br>Requires integration work to be completed at the leadership level |
| **2. Geography**<br>*Organized around physical locations, such as states, countries, or regions* | Enables local focus and customization and relationships with active local governments<br>Reduces transportation costs | Can be difficult to mobilize and share resources across regional boundaries |
| **3. Product**<br>*Organized into product divisions, each with its own functional structure to support product lines* | Can shorten product development cycles, and enables "state-of-the-art" research<br>Locates profit and loss responsibility for each product at the division level with a general manager<br>Possibly develops positive team identity around product lines with clear line of sight between decisions and success of business | May lead to divergence among product lines in focus and standards<br>Encourages loyalty to product division, which may make it hard to recognize when a product should be changed or dropped<br>Can cause duplication of resources and functions<br>Loses economies of scale when functions are spread out<br>Creates multiple points of contact for the customer |
| **4. Customer**<br>*Organized around major market segments, such as client groups, industries, or population groups* | Makes it easy to customize for customers through in-depth relationships and customer loyalty<br>Enables value-added product and service bundles and solutions, avoiding commoditized products and competition on price alone | Causes divergence among customer and market segments in focus and standards, as well as duplication of resources and functions<br>Requires an ability to track customer profitability |

basis for choosing the best strategic grouping. An analysis must be done against the capabilities that are essential to executing the specific business strategy. In the previous chapters, we defined capabilities and their importance as the criteria against which all design decisions are made. We also introduced design drivers as a framework for analyzing the current organization. We can now use the design drivers as a tool to evaluate the design options against the criteria. To illustrate, we'll focus our discussion here on a capability that many companies struggle to build and maintain: *innovation*, or the ability to develop new products and services faster than the competition. For reference, a summary of the design drivers is shown in Table 5.2.

All CEOs are under pressure to find sustainable sources of organic growth. But a study of a thousand companies found no significant relationship between R&D spending and sales, earnings growth, profitability, or shareholder returns (Jaruzelski, Dehoff, and Bordia, 2005). Successful innovation in large companies requires more than throwing money at the problem. Rather, innovation depends on organizational arrangements that build distinct capabilities that allow the company to generate new ideas, assess and develop concepts, then move them quickly into the market. When the goal is breakthrough innovation (creating truly new products rather than extensions of established offerings), those capabilities are all the more difficult to build.

Structure is certainly not the only element in creating an innovation capability, but it is a good place to start. The six design drivers are a lens for understanding how a variety of organizational groupings can help build capabilities in new product innovation. Let's examine each of the design drivers and look at examples of design decisions made in a range of companies as a way to illustrate the how different strategic grouping choices can all support a path to enhancing innovation.

TABLE 5.2. *Summary of the Six Design Drivers*

| | |
|---|---|
| Management attention | • Forces attention to critical imperatives<br>• Elevates an organizational component in the hierarchy<br>• *Examples*: Emerging-markets executive, incubators for new product development, functional "czar" for a new process |
| Leveraged resources and cost | • Creates economies of scale through the concentration of like activities (for cost management and efficiency)<br>• Includes centralized and central-led corporate activities<br>• Includes flat and lean structures<br>• *Example*: Shared service center |
| Coordination and integration | • Ties things together into a "whole" outcome, end-to-end<br>• Can be delivered through structural and nonstructural solutions—often process based<br>• Allows for another dimension of decision making laterally across the organization<br>• *Examples*: Product management team, global category team, brand management council |
| Specialization | • Differentiates or separates out a role or group by expertise or functional activity<br>• Ensures technical excellence—centers of expertise<br>• *Example*: Central R&D function serving multiple product lines |
| Control and accountability | • Is often an outcome of simplicity and clarity of reporting<br>• Elevates or centralizes problem issues to ensure that they are controlled<br>• *Examples*: Quality reporting to the top executive, product divisions with full accountability under a general manager |
| Learning and motivation | • Provides high degrees of authority and accountability on a relatively small scale, to allow risk-taking<br>• Provides diverse challenges, including exposure to international environments<br>• *Examples*: Small P&L units created to grow future general managers; rotational assignments, project roles |

### Management Attention

One way to spur innovation is to give it greater management attention and visibility. The people responsible for leading innovation report at a high level of the organization. Many companies struggle with deciding which projects to fund and how to allocate scarce resources across innovation opportunities. In a world of incremental product extensions, today's leaders are encouraged by higher management to be bolder and to fund fewer, bigger bets. Leaders who want to ensure that the right choices are made and who want to encourage risk-taking in the organization know that their best and most senior players need to invest personal leadership time and attention in the hard work of innovation.

This is the case at Nike, where a global senior vice president for design reports directly to the COO, as a peer to the major business units. Shawcor Ltd., a Canadian energy services company that delivers coating and protection solutions for oil and gas pipelines, has grown an average of 15 percent a year for nearly a decade by constantly finding new solutions to very difficult problems faced by the world's major oil companies. The CEO at Shawcor has elevated a chief innovation officer to report to him and made certain that updates on new product development are part of the monthly executive routines in the company.

Using management attention to grow a needed capability starts with structure and roles that send the message "this work is important" and is then supported by the right processes, metrics, and talent. For example, the chief executive at Nike personally reviews creative ideas from designers and material tech people. He is often seen sketching ideas in interaction with his chief design officer. Top leaders across the company are as passionate about product esthetics and performance as they are about sports. At Shawcor, the CEO and each of his division general managers, in this nearly $2 billion company, personally work with customers and internal technical people to find new fixes to stubborn problems. A GM at Shawcor doesn't hesitate to stand at a bench with pieces of scrap pipe, foam rubber, tape, or fabrics, jerry-rigging prototypes. Such behaviors are encouraged and rewarded.

### Leveraged Resources and Cost

Leverage is a type of specialization and management attention, specifically focused on increasing the return on investments a company has already made in people, brands, and physical assets. The purpose of this design driver is cost-effective use of limited resources and preserving capabilities that are difficult to create.

A typical example of a leveraged unit is a centralized shared service center. The benefits of such a design choice are economies of scale, ability to invest in high levels of expertise, and the ability to drive common process. But leverage is often directly opposed to breaking work into the smaller, divisional units that are beneficial to motivating people and defining clear units of accountability.

A common problem is that the budgets of centralized functions must be allocated back to the operating units, which may cloud accountability, especially when some units are more inclined to utilize the central resources than others. Further, distance from customers, the bureaucratic tendencies of large consolidated resource pools, and isolation from the cadence of the business can reduce responsiveness and creativity.

Leverage is not typically a design driver emphasized in companies focused on innovation. The track record of large, centralized R&D groups is spotty in many multibusiness companies. But investment in pools of highly specialized skills should be leveraged. In divisionalized companies, one attractive opportunity for leverage is advanced development—the research side of R&D. Some kinds of talent and skills are simply too difficult to acquire and retain, and even the largest firm can't afford to have them scattered about. Bringing basic research into a centralized group is a common and effective form of leverage.

Another way in which leverage can be used to support innovation is to group together nonstrategic, but necessary, activities and manage them for efficiency and cost. This can free up resources to invest in the experiments, trials, and inevitable failures that characterize effective innovation.

### Coordination and Integration

Separated and specialized product innovation initiatives must be linked back into the operating business at important interfaces. This integration can be achieved through dedicated roles or units, through process, or through shared metrics and rewards. For example, if a new product set is going to rely on the strengths of established distribution channels, it must be designed to be successful in those channels. The risk of launching new products developed outside the mainstream of the business (overemphasizing management attention or specialization) is that they may be rejected by the sales organization, not supported with marketing programs, or not serviced effectively by technical support units in the field. When this happens, the new business has no more advantage than a start-up. Specialization, without integration at some level, undermines the benefits provided by the core company.

Moore (2005) describes the challenge of the "adolescent" business, the emerging business with perhaps $20 million to

$200 million in revenue, inside the context of the larger corporation. He argues that these businesses can be gradually integrated into the core, but only if they are given their own measures of revenue, and perhaps margin, with no expectation for profit contribution or operations excellence.

McKesson has maintained separately focused health care technology business units and is not eager to integrate them quickly. It does this in order to accelerate the pace of product development among very specialized applications in health care. But these complex solutions must be linked back to a common sales and marketing organization in order to leverage the company's substantial scale and influence among major health care customers. And, increasingly, customers are asking for McKesson's patient script management, billing systems, and hospital HR solutions to be tied together into an integrated systems architecture. Finding the balance of specialization and integration is a difficult task for units like McKesson's technical solutions center. Large customers have started to demand more integration. But 90 percent of the division's revenue is still from legacy products. So the organization must realign to gradually manage new, integrated solutions while maintaining adequate focus on the older, established ones, a challenge for many companies that are evolving to systems solutions.

### Specialization

A variation of management attention, particularly in large companies, is to separate innovation activities from the core work of the business—to specialize innovation work (DeGraff and Quinn, 2007; Govindarajan and Trimble, 2005; Kates and Galbraith, 2007). New product platforms are often pulled out of established business units and given peer status so that they will not be lost in the competition for resources and management attention. Platforms involving unproven technologies may need even greater separation to avoid the effects of management behaviors aimed at protecting core technologies that are threatened by new ones. This separation, with links back to the existing business where needed, allows for focus and specialization. Those working on the new products and services are allowed to diverge, unencumbered by the strictures on how the core work is conducted.

As an example, juices, waters, and teas were latecomers to Coca-Cola's global portfolio of brands and categories. Finding their way into the stream dominated by carbonated soft drinks, with their massive sales and very attractive margins, was a major challenge. In local markets around the world, numerous smaller successes had occurred over many years but had never been leveraged. Ultimately the fix that gave these new sources of growth higher priority in the global portfolio at Coke was to create peer-level business units for these categories and brands, separate from the core, even though their revenue was dwarfed by the carbonated soft drink business. The new businesses take the form of highly specialized units focused on new beverage development. Category leaders have their own separate development people assigned by tech centers that specialize in juice, water, tea, or coffee.

Coke creates further specialization within the development community by assigning one of the geographically based development centers a specific role to play in the larger new product development agenda and network. The geographic technical centers remain somewhat decentralized in reporting relationships, but each has a clear, assigned responsibility to be the global center of expertise for a given drink platform—based largely on established track records of achievement. For example teas are, not surprisingly, the specialty of the Shanghai development center.

Specialization drives focus, often at the expense of integration. Success at Apple stems from the meticulous care and feeding of a specific group—the creatives—who receive organizational placement high in the structure (management attention). These software developers are managed in very separate organizations at Apple. No one in any of these segmented units can see the entire picture. Secrecy and control of information are the norm. One observer notes, "Apple's creatives have no more insight into the company's overall operations than an Army private has into the Pentagon" (Morrison, 2009). At the same time, these specialized groups have their own highly secured work area intended to reproduce the feeling of a small design firm, free of all interruptions. Apple's organizational approach allows it to coddle its most valuable, productive employees and is one of the company's most formidable assets. Integration, therefore, has to occur at a high level. Decisions related to innovation often involve the CEO, Steve Jobs, and his direct reports.

Apple illustrates that there is no particular structure that is best to build a particular capability. Apple is a large and successful innovator that is mostly organized around highly specialized functional units. Strategic grouping at the highest level includes a senior vice president for design, another for software engineering, one for applications, another for retail, and another for worldwide marketing. Jobs's COO manages another set of mostly functional leaders. The structure is relatively simple. Apple's leaders have made the design decision to emphasize focus and specialization and to manage integration at very senior levels. This approach has worked for them.

### Control and Accountability

Placing control and accountability at the right level also impacts the development of capabilities. Most organizations are reconfigured into divisions as soon as they grow beyond a simple single-product-line business. The essential purpose of the division is to break down the complexity of the organization into manageable and controllable units. Each unit is typically led by a general manager.

Many companies hold innovation as a value and a goal, yet are challenged to achieve the results they desire. When everyone is responsible for the outcome, then no one is. The leader asks, "Whom do I hold accountable for innovation?" The temptation to assign an innovation officer at the top (for management attention) must be balanced with the need to keep division GMs accountable for the growth of their businesses. This can be a delicate balance. We gave the example of Coca-Cola creating specialized centers of expertise for coffee, tea, and juices. But Coke's management chose not to centralize the global product development organization precisely because it wanted its regional presidents to remain accountable for product creation in their markets. It has chosen, rather, to link those efforts through a formalized communication network, a common innovation process, and a coordinated set of development priorities. In this way, Coke has used specialization to create focus on new product development and integration mechanisms to foster global linkages, but has balanced this by leaving accountability metrics for the success of the business overall largely with the regions. This design has created a dynamic global conversation and the desired innovation. Managing the balance of power in this design becomes the work of leadership.

### Learning and Motivation

Cisco's emerging technologies group was formed in 2006 and has proven itself a successful incubator and accelerator for new businesses even through a down economy. Such a structure is an example of management attention (grouping and elevating small-revenue units into a highly visible component of the company to protect them from the core business). Many companies use this mechanism. Cisco's advantage, however, has been in creating an environment of learning, sharing, and collaboration—all of which are behaviors essential to creating an innovation capability. From this environment come the ideas and projects that populate the incubator.

Cisco's CEO, John Chambers, began to shape a culture of enterprise-wide creativity and collaboration with a massive restructuring shortly after the tech bust of 2001. He created "distributed innovation" networks and boards, which now deliver 70 percent of the company's innovations. His objective was to "reduce organization dependency on himself and other senior executives" (McGirt, 2009, p. 88). He is convinced that real innovation is possible only when people in diverse functions, P&L units, and markets are empowered to collaborate together and with customers. Anyone with a good idea may receive funding and a small team of cross-functional resources. The process is often described as chaotic, even anarchic. But the goal—new products—is clear, and the informal confederations of technologists and others have been set loose to find them. In many ways this approach is the opposite of Apple's, yet it is just as successful.

What this discussion has illustrated is that there are many ways to build an innovation capability. Doing so is more complex than choosing one structure over another. The unit's leadership has to make conscious choices among options. The design drivers framework is a useful way of defining and evaluating the options.

# Choose the Best Grouping Option

C HOOSING THE BEST ALTERNATIVE FROM AMONG the classic design options is the core task of strategic grouping. There is no single right answer to the puzzle; the key is to select the option that delivers the most benefits with the fewest risks.

The work begins by laying out some hypotheses about which options best support the capabilities you are trying to create. We recommend that leaders define at least two high-level options (or hypotheses) and then test them by calling out the likely benefits and risks of each. We often start with "bubble" diagrams that help show relationships among component parts that might come together in a design. If we want to consider organizing around markets, for example, we will create bubbles for those markets, with headers that serve as placeholders. We can then consider what other major load-bearing units might be part of this option. Figure 6.1 illustrates an early design hypothesis for an industrial products company, focused on customer groups. We hypothesize in the example that products must be managed across the customer-facing units and that a "back end" is needed to manage shared manufacturing sites.

FIGURE 6.1. *Sample Bubble Diagram of an Early Design Hypothesis for an Industrial Products Company, Focused on Customer Groups*

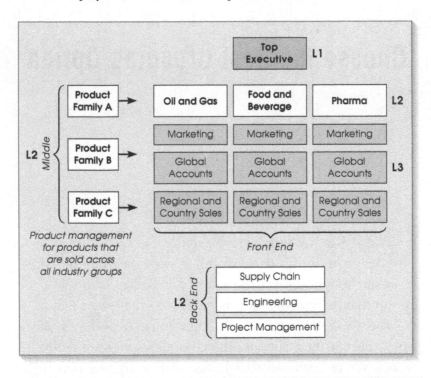

Generating and evaluating strategic grouping options is an iterative process. Organizations are multilayered, and it is very difficult to understand the pros and cons of a given option without imagining at least two layers deep. We cannot debate the benefits of the customer-centric units in our bubble diagram without having some idea what the work is inside these units. We hypothesize that each customer unit might have its own marketing, account management, and the like. Now it is easier to debate the pros and cons of the customer-centric option.

To take the point further, let's refer to the leader in our design as L1 (for level one); her direct reports are L2, and so on. The classic design choices will look different from one level to the next. If the L2 choice is to align by markets, then L3 could be aligned by functional units; or it could be aligned by submarkets or even geographic units. And a given level could be organized around more than one classic option, depending on the work. The key is to find ways to blend and balance the strengths and weaknesses of the varied options in terms of the six design drivers. If we gain the benefits of customer integration at L2, then we may need to reinforce functional excellence at the next level down by organizing L3 by function in order to gain specialization.

There is no value in purity. A complex strategy will result in some complexity of organization. Although simplicity is a virtue, leaders should avoid simplicity that is aimed at making their jobs easier, when a more complex formation is likely to capture more value.

Once a number of strategic grouping options are laid out and two or three are identified as preferred, then it will make sense to go deeper into the details of how to organize L3 and L4. It varies by project, but often L3 is the extent of practical detail that can be considered during the Strategic Grouping phase. Subsequent levels of design are more likely to occur inside the Integration phase, using a bottom-up view (based on a detailed picture of the work) conducted by separate work streams for each group. This is the most effective approach in many design projects.

When a grouping option is considered, such as the customer-centric example in Figure 6.1, it will usually have several components to it. We think it is important to be able to describe the overall design option without the use of organization charts. Here is an example of a verbal description of an early design concept:

*Reporting to the general manager will be a set of vertical market units and product families. These units will have dedicated marketing functions and will go to market through a geographic sales and service organization supported by a shared supply chain organization.*

We have now blended design options into a "design concept." At this early point in the design work, it is just that—a concept. We are looking for at least two such viable concepts before any decisions are made. Often it is best to keep an alternative design concept alive as you test your preferred option.

## ORGANIZATIONAL ARCHETYPES

Are there rules of thumb that suggest that one form of grouping is likely to be more effective for a given industry? On the basis of his studies of business life cycles, innovation expert Geoffrey Moore (2005) argues that there are two broad types of businesses that require two very different forms of organizational architecture. He describes the opposing nature of *complex systems* companies and *volume operations* companies. The former (think IBM, Cisco, Goldman Sachs, Boeing, and Bechtel) tackle complex business problems with highly individualized solutions that blend products and services and bring them to a handful of very big customers. Volume operations businesses, by contrast (think Verizon, P&G, Nike, Hertz, and Target), serve volume markets, usually consumers, with a variety of standardized offers, involving millions of transactions. Moore argues that the shape of the customer base (very narrow in complex systems companies, very wide in the volume operations businesses) informs organization architecture. The economics of serving a few hundred or perhaps a few thousand customers as opposed to tens of millions must be considered. In the complex systems model, the customer can and should be the center of highly integrated activities all aimed at elaborate courtship and the delivery of complex solutions. In the volume operations industries, the core activity is differentiated, cost-effective production.

These archetypes require different capabilities. Moore's first archetype of business must be very good at integrated solutions and account management; his second, broadly speaking, must compete through selection, availability, and price. The first interacts through individualized contact, the second through brand messaging and media. If we apply the six design drivers and extrapolate the kind of strategic grouping that is likely to fit each of the two business types, the logic might look something as shown in Figure 6.2.

FIGURE 6.2. *Two Archetypical Businesses and the Typical Implications for Requisite Capabilities, Design Drivers, and Strategic Grouping*

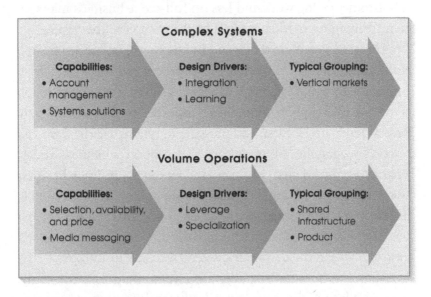

*Source:* Adapted from Moore, 2005

Broad archetypes like Moore's should not be taken as prescriptions, and there are many variations within each, especially in companies that are ambidextrous and try to combine these two models. However, we find it a powerful idea that can help in developing early design hypotheses.

## NEW APPROACHES TO GEOGRAPHIC ORGANIZATION

For businesses that must organize into geographic regions, it can be helpful to have some frameworks for thinking about how to use location as an organizing principle. Geography remains the preferred option in many companies for organizing customer-facing activities like account management, sales, and service. Increasingly globalization has narrowed the scope of country-based subsidiaries of global corporations and groups, focusing them more on customer-facing work and less on full-scope business management. Emerging markets are often the exception, however.

The traditional methods of dividing geographic units into modified continents have changed in recent years, due largely to greater reliance on offshore markets for growth; the concentration of major growth opportunities in a handful of markets, such Brazil, Russia, India, and China; and pressure to rationalize the overhead costs of geographic infrastructure and support activities. Today, separate countries may or may not represent optimal business footprints, and traditional continental groupings are often too big and lacking in any real rationale for organizational focus. Regional headquarters are often viewed internally as more bureaucratic and controlling than the corporate center, especially in Europe.

Many companies are adjusting their maps continuously, gerrymandering larger and smaller footprints around available management talent. This isn't necessarily a bad thing, but a set of design criteria should be considered; ignoring some of the factors that are specific to effective geographic coverage may suboptimize results.

As we have seen, geography is especially useful in creating high degrees of management attention and coverage in local markets. It is also very effective for placing local control and accountability where the people and assets are located, which is why it remains a core design principle for many global players. It can also provide coordination and integration at the local level.

The pros and cons of various groupings of geographic units can be understood most effectively with the benefit of a set of specific criteria. There are a number of these that we have found quite useful in thinking through how to align geographic boundaries into organization. The importance of these criteria depends entirely on the business. Some may be critical and others irrelevant.

- Emerging market focus
- Optimization of geographic portfolio management
- Cultural, language, and geopolitical adjacencies
- External partner structures and location
- Concentration of revenue, people, and assets

### Emerging Market Focus

Emerging markets with high growth potential benefit from focus and management attention. IBM realigned three developing-markets groups within Americas; Asia; and the Middle East, Africa, and Eastern Europe. These small-revenue markets were projected in 2008 to deliver growth at a rate of 21 percent of current sales. Focus and management attention are key. CEO Sam Palmisano made the argument in an interview with the *Wall Street Journal* that he did not want the ongoing challenges in established markets like Japan, Germany, and the United States to steal management time from these key growth targets (Bulkeley, 2008).

It is clear that the capabilities that are necessary to manage highly sophisticated consumer markets in Europe and North America, such as marketing, are very different from those needed in high-growth markets like India and China. There is a pace, a rhythm, and a set of best practices that are easier to manage with consistency among like geographic units. It is also easier to select leaders who are better motivational and skill fits for one market type or another. Some companies actively manage career paths to give high-potential leaders exposure to multiple market types precisely because of the differences among them.

### Optimization of Geographic Portfolio Management

Many companies actively manage investments on the basis of their geographic portfolios. Companies that invest heavily in direct marketing, for example, will routinely reduce advertising spending in one or more countries in order to increase the spending in others so as to maximize the impact on quarterly or annual business results. Others may make similar choices over the longer term by starving investment in sales or production capability in one geographic unit that appears to have less growth potential in order to fund others.

This form of operational portfolio management makes sense when it is governed at the right level by people who are being measured on the right results and time frames. It is smart design to consider where and under what circumstances these trade-off decisions should be made. Geographic clusters can be set to encourage the general manager of the unit to optimize the results of the overall footprint by shifting resources across subunits in a way that does not sell out the future of the business in highly prized geographic units that may take longer to develop.

We have seen smart clustering of cash-generating countries like the United Kingdom and France, for example, together with fast-growth countries such as South Africa, with the intent of taking cash out of the former to build brands in the latter.

### *Cultural, Language, and Geopolitical Adjacencies*

There have always been logical groupings shaped by culture and history. In breaking the Middle East and Africa into subgroups, some companies are deliberate in keeping the more liberal and largely French-speaking North and West African countries clustered together, while linking Egypt, for example, to the Middle East. The long, strained history between Japan and Korea still causes many companies to avoid grouping the two together, unless they are part of a much larger geographic unit.

### *External Partner Structures and Location*

The location and nature of external partners can influence the way a business aligns geographic units. In businesses that rely heavily on third-party distribution, colocation of internal resources with the external partner may be quite beneficial. The capabilities needed to run this kind of third-party distribution business are oriented toward marketing and franchise management, not direct selling. Geographic units can be quite large.

As an example, large beer and soft drink distributors in Spain and France own extensive networks of bottling plants, distribution hubs, and people all over North and West Africa. Companies like Coca-Cola pay attention to those geographic footprints in aligning their own internal organizational boundaries in order to create simple, aligned connections between their own local franchise management and marketing centers and the bottler territories for production, sales, and distribution. The partnerships are well served by these alignments and colocation arrangements.

### Concentration of Revenue, People, and Assets

Leverage calls for finding efficient clusters for managing so-called backroom operations. Many companies have created pan-European service centers for administrative activities. These activities do not necessarily have to correspond to the same boundaries that are used for the operating units, especially if they are managed by center-based functions.

These administratively focused, geography-based units can be managed separately from the operating units. This is especially useful when multiple divisions operate independently within a given region. A senior executive is assigned a "landlord" role to

- Harmonize approaches to people management across businesses (including works council interface)
- Manage all matters related to local regulatory and political entities
- Manage expense and capital budgets for shared service activities
- Administer contracts, procedures, and purchase agreements

These administrative or landlord roles can be held as a "second hat" for an operator, or can be full-time administrative assignments. They may or may not retain the "country manager" title.

Some companies segment geographic markets by sales volume in order to determine the most effective groupings. One of our client companies recently sorted the 115 countries in which it does business into four buckets, based purely on revenue growth plans, ranging from megamarket countries to very small ones. Having done this, the company was able to apply some analytics to determine which should be stand-alone markets with a senior executive, and which needed to be clustered. It also used the four buckets to set guidelines for the kind of infrastructure that was needed in-country as opposed to at the cluster level. In so doing it was able to completely shed the legacy and expense of regional headquarters and replace them with a flatter set of clusters. The small countries were identified as territories that were staffed only with salespeople; medium countries were aggregated with others of the same size and provided minimal marketing resources along with salespeople; large countries were designated as possible single-market entities or anchor countries inside clusters that were staffed with marketing, support, and category managers; and the megamarket countries retained SBU responsibility and were fully staffed accordingly (see Table 6.1).

TABLE 6.1. *Segmenting Countries by Revenue to Determine Cluster Rules and Resource Requirements in a Consumer Products Company*

|  | *< $100m*<br>*Small* | *$100m–$400m*<br>*Medium* | *$400m–$1b*<br>*Large* | *> $1b*<br>*Megamarket* |
|---|---|---|---|---|
| **Principles** | • Sales territory<br>• Led by sales director | • Aggregated with other geographic units if possible | • Single market entity<br>• May be combined with other geographic units into a cluster | • May be managed as a single entity or be segmented into multiple business units |
| **Organization** | • Sales | • Sales<br>• Marketing | • Sales<br>• Marketing<br>• Merchandising<br>• Limited category staff | • Sales<br>• Marketing-Merchandising<br>• Full category staff<br>• Support staff<br>• SBU metrics |

## When Options Appear Equally Valid

When two or more strategic grouping options appear to be equally valid, there are other criteria that you can consider. It is useful to return to the business case and insights from the assessment process. We suggest a simple set of tests.

### Degree of Change

Your organization's starting point determines the degree of change. In general, you want to achieve results with the least amount of change and disruption. For example, creating an integrative brand management role that works across existing operating units is one way to build a brand capability. Such a role requires a sophisticated set of influence and interpersonal skills in the brand leaders. It also requires managers in the operating units to cede some authority to the new role. In an organization that already is adept at using cross-functional teams and has models for such integrative roles, the brand manager role may represent a small degree of change. In another company, where the operating units have had a high degree of autonomy and little experience with such roles, brand management may introduce a huge change. A lighter touch—such as networks or teams—may be a less disruptive, albeit less high-impact, way to start on the road to brand capability.

### Primacy

A long list of capabilities may be important over the long term, but there is likely to be a hierarchy of importance in the short term. Priorities among the capabilities will guide the sequence in which you make strategic grouping decisions. For example, a finance unit may need to add more specialized decision support roles. It will also need to create common processes to reduce costs. The first step is often to focus on consolidating transactional activities into regional shared services, in order to free up resources that can then be repurposed into advisory roles.

### Management's Capacity for Complexity

An elegant design solution on paper is worthless if the management team does not have the wherewithal to execute it. The ability of leadership teams to manage complex organizational forms takes time to develop. Building these skills is easier with a team that (1) has worked together and built strong working relationships, (2) is made up of members who come from other companies that are successful in managing complex organizations, and (3) has some track record of shared accountability and decision making. Management time is expensive. You may be better off with a design that has some duplication of less expensive resources, rather than a seemingly efficient design that will consume costly management time in internal negotiations.

### Biggest Impact

As you analyze your options, ask which will yield the biggest impact. The work of organization design is hard and distracting regardless of the scale. If you are going to make a change, choose that which will not only fix today's problem but move the organization significantly forward.

### Most Visible to Customers

Test that the option is solving a customer or other stakeholder need, not just a management need. Leaders will sometimes gravitate to what seems easiest to manage, rather than to what will have the biggest impact. The design should make the organization easy for customers and employees to navigate—the managers' job is to negotiate the complexity of interfaces.

### Fits the Existing Culture

Some options fit the existing way of doing business better than others. If your organization has a distinct culture that is a strength you want to preserve, choose options that work best with the culture.

### Forces a Change to the Existing Culture

Conversely, if the assessment has shown that the current culture is an obstacle to future success, then you may need a design that very visibly changes the patterns of decision making and signals a new way of working.

A company can shift focus of resources in order to drive new behaviors and capabilities. As an illustration, McKesson has found success, in the past, through strategic grouping that emphasizes management attention, specialization, and control. It had been primarily organized into business units focused on different health care product families, each with a strong general manager. Customers, however, are starting to seek information solutions from across McKesson's business units, forcing the company to shift strategy and begin to focus more on integration of common technical platforms. Getting software and information services developers to work together around a common platform is often very difficult.

One option for McKesson would be to retain separate applications development units, each highly focused on its own product line (for example, invoicing, script management, and human resource utilization), connected by a development network or council. This option will be appealing to the current general managers because the number of orders for the "integrated solution" is small relative to the existing business. But integrated solutions that truly cut across these applications won't happen by chance—they require strong linkage across the units or perhaps even the formation of a single, integrated solutions business unit. In the future, McKesson is likely to evolve toward fewer profit centers. This option will probably be poorly received by the general managers, as no one will be eager to lose the accountability and control of their smaller, separate units any sooner than she has to. An interim option would be to add a chief technology officer role that can force an integrated approach, while leaving the underlying business unit structure intact.

# Embrace the Matrix

I N STRATEGIC GROUPING, OUR GOAL IS TO IDENTIFY basic organizational units that will carry the strategic work forward. But what happens when there is more than one strategic load to bear? The answer is the matrix.

A *matrix* is the combination of two or more of the building blocks into equally important dimensions. The matrix creates multiple reporting relationships that force managers to pay attention to two or more sets of sometimes competing objectives. As Galbraith (2009) points out, conflict in the matrix is evidence that it is working and that diverse points of view are being considered.

Most commonly a matrix is used to provide specific decision rights to centralized functional departments in an otherwise simple line of business or geographic organization structure. This allows the business to achieve the benefits of two design drivers: far-flung geographic units receive effective management attention, and at the same time economies of scale are leveraged in the centralized functional activities. Another common example of the matrix is the company that seeks to build one or more brands across geographic units; a matrix is used to create global accountability for the brand while execution is left in the geographic units. Figure 7.1 illustrates the basic concept of the matrix.

Conflict in a matrix is guaranteed, not because people aren't willing to work together, but because objectives are often at odds. For example, maximizing geographic revenue and profit may undermine efforts to create common positioning for a brand across regions. Even though this tension can slow decision making, it is only by forcing the trade-off discussion through the matrix that both objectives receive attention. Simple structures are usually not adequate for complex work.

A balanced matrix exists when two or more axes of the organization are essentially equal in power. This does not mean that all decisions are shared; one dimension may have authority over another for a given set of decisions (for example, what advertising

FIGURE 7.1. *A Typical Matrix Organization*

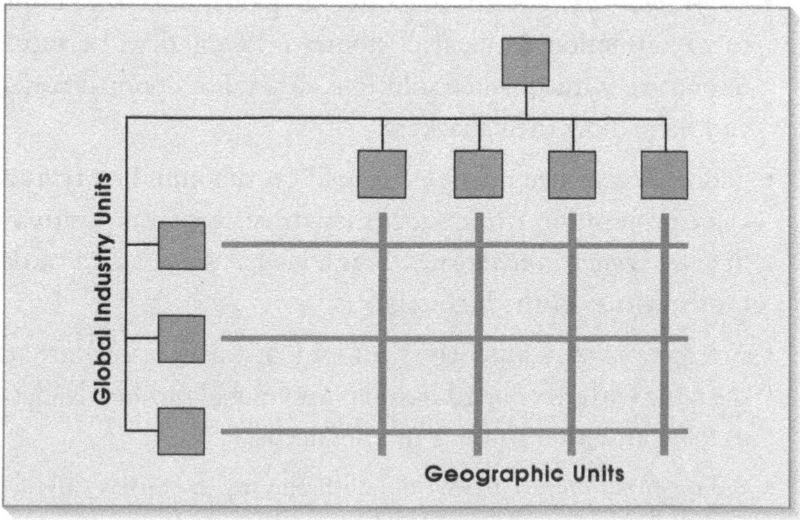

agency will be used) while the other has authority over another set of decisions (for example, direct marketing spend). A matrix does force collaborative decision making around some shared objectives. It is a team-based organization.

Although many managers would choose to avoid the complexity of the matrix, it is clear that today's global organizations cannot usually be effective without sharing power across two or more roles in the matrix. More important, tension in the matrix is not in itself a bad thing. Tension is inherent in today's complex business strategies, and most large multinationals must find a way to make the tension work for shareholders. It is often the only way to make human and financial capital fully productive. When companies like Procter & Gamble or Nokia succeed in managing the complexity of their organizations, they achieve competitive advantage because competitors cannot easily copy these structures (Galbraith, 2009).

Following is a list of some of the matrix tensions that exist in many large companies today:

- *Geographic units* keep pressure on global business units to pay attention to local customer needs and to be more responsive with quicker solutions. They are opportunistic, and they know their markets.

- Global *brands* keep people focused on the brand story and value proposition worldwide; they drive common positioning and bigger innovations. Brand leaders serve as stewards for the future of the business.

- *Emerging market* executives (in China, for example) are at the table with developed markets and global product leaders to force attention to their unique needs.

- A *cross-functional* team works with the top executives inside a global customer organization, with a single voice, as a condition of being a tier-one supplier to whom the customer will outsource inventory solutions.

- A critical global *function* makes certain that technical skill sets meet the standard required in all businesses and that the overall cost of these skills is competitive.

- *Business development* teams are tasked with making certain that new growth platforms get adequate attention and funding to thrive as the source of innovation alongside the core business.

## MAKING STRATEGIC GROUPING CHOICES IN A MATRIX

The matrix takes many forms. At Colgate-Palmolive, the primary axis is regional and country profit centers, with brand and category networks used to coordinate across the geographic structures. P&G, in contrast, has organized around categories and has realigned geographic units and functions to coordinate across these product lines.

The design and implementation of matrix structures is a topic well covered in recent books (Galbraith, 2009; Kates and Galbraith, 2007). We think it's useful to distinguish three types of matrix structures for purposes of illustrating some core options for strategic grouping. These three broad types can be considered on a continuum of complexity. We will examine them in sequence, from the relatively simple to the quite complex, with an emphasis on how the six design drivers might inform one of these matrix choices.

### Matrix Type 1: Function Versus Business Unit

This relatively simple matrix can be found in most multibusiness companies today. Business units are configured to serve a specific market at a profit. General managers are given clear control and accountability over the business unit. However, the functional staff inside each business unit often has a corporate or group counterpart that oversees their work on some basis. This oversight serves to tie the function staff to a common agenda that cuts across business units. For example, a division finance manager nearly always has a second boss in the corporate finance department, as do most human resources managers, IT leaders, and leaders in other functions.

This type of matrix creates tension between the drivers of coordination and integration and of control and accountability. The functions are charged with integrating and linking. This comes into conflict with the general manager's desire for autonomy and authority to make all decisions in the business unit. Despite this tension, this matrix dynamic is not a difficult one to manage. The roles between business units and functions are relatively easy to sort, and decision rights can be parsed among them without great difficulty. If the operating model for the business is a closely related set of business units, then the functions will likely have more power in decision making in the business units. If the business units do not have much in common, then there is no reason for the functions to push for strong integration. Power relationships, which we will examine in great detail in Milestone Three, should be spelled out for the functions and business units in a manner consistent with the operating model.

### Matrix Type 2: Front End (Geographic Unit or Customer) Versus Back End (Product or Function)

A second common type of matrix is the front-back organization. This type of matrix is recommended when there is a need to place management attention on key market segments on the one hand, and a need to leverage capital-intensive operations on the other.

There are real benefits in organizing commercial activities around customers or consumers and giving them management attention. But often companies seek the simultaneous benefits of leverage and efficiency in those activities that are not customer facing. The strategic grouping solution is to split the front end and the back end: to tie all the customer-facing functions together into an integrated business team, often with a P&L; and at the same time, pool the back-end functions that need to be managed more on the basis of leverage, cost-effectiveness, and specialized skill sets. In this way, opposing design drivers coexist in a matrix.

This is a more challenging matrix to manage. The back end is half of the business. It typically manages most of the people and the assets, and owns key elements of the P&L, including profit margin on products or solutions. The front end owns the customer and must execute all commercial activities. It has top-line revenue accountability in the P&L. Power must be balanced between the two consistent with the capabilities that are sought. It is useful to be very clear that the back end acts as service provider to the front end in satisfying customer needs. Having said that, in order to gain the benefits of leverage and efficiency, supply chain leaders must have powerful votes in such decisions as procurement, sourcing, and the overall manufacturing footprint of the business.

### Matrix Type 3: Global Customer or Product Line Versus Local Geographic Unit

A third common form of matrix is employed in the company that seeks the simultaneous benefits of attention to local customers (with local empowerment) and global customers or product focus (with greater integration). This is the most challenging matrix to govern. Geography is usually the dominant force in these structures, by design or happenstance. It is the legacy of any company that has grown by planting flags around the world, empowering local managers to compete and grow the business as they see fit in order to gain a toehold in a new market. It is the nature of people to identify with place, with home. Local might mean you are from Milano; it might mean you are Italian; or it might mean you are a European, depending on what entity is trying to influence you toward some larger agenda.

There are high degrees of tension in this matrix because both the horizontal (global customer or product) and vertical (geographic) axes own commercial work. They may own overlapping elements of profit and loss, and they may both claim they own the customer or the consumer. This matrix becomes quite complex when three or more dimensions are in play, including product or solutions, customer, geography, function, and brand.

Most global companies have retained a matrix that is tipped to the geographic axis, perhaps because of the challenges of a truly balanced matrix. When the matrix is balanced, decisions tend to be escalated to higher levels of management, so it is easier to give the geographic units 51 percent of the vote. But the balanced product-geographic matrix can be the right choice when senior leadership wants to be actively involved in making the trade-off decisions. In today's volatile markets, this kind of direct executive involvement in trading off the benefits of investing in a global ad campaign (think integration) against fast, responsive experiments with consumers in India (think local empowerment and motivation) may be time well spent.

The balanced matrix is only a good strategic grouping choice when both sets of drivers are critical to achieve the capabilities or design criteria. Positioning a global business unit as an equal partner to geographic market units requires real confidence in the strategy on the part of leadership.

## CASE EXAMPLE: USING STRATEGIC GROUPING TO BUILD MULTIPLE CAPABILITIES

Few companies have the luxury to organize so as to optimize just one capability. The case we discuss here serves as an example of the thought process for strategic grouping decisions made in relation to a broader set of capabilities that must be balanced against one another. The case company is the same one referenced in Chapter Six.

V&C Ltd. is a $4 billion, U.S.-based manufacturer of industrial valves and controls for customers around the world. It was formed largely through a series of acquisitions of small firms based in Europe, North America, and the Pacific. The company was organized into these three geographic regions reflecting its history as a collection of local firms, as shown in Figure 7.2.

In 2008, a new president was charged with revising V&C's strategy and organization. Although the company was profitable, a number of factors were inhibiting future growth:

- An increase in global customers and complex cross-border projects
- A need for more product innovation linked closely to industry-specific needs
- An inability to devote resources to emerging and new markets

The new president put forward four primary growth paths:

1. Build deep customer relationships in five vertical industries (oil and gas, nuclear power, chemicals, mining, and water)
2. Leverage the breadth of existing product offerings into these vertical industries

FIGURE 7.2. *V&C Ltd. Legacy Organization, with Geographic Strategic Grouping of Autonomous Subsidiary (Acquired) Businesses*

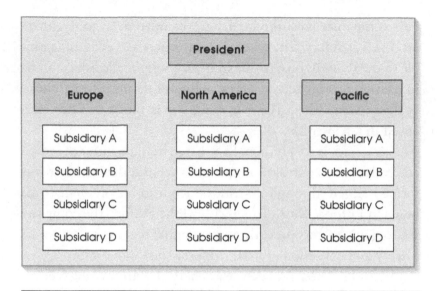

3. Ensure a life-cycle approach to new product development and build professional and technical service capabilities to provide high-value customer solutions
4. Accelerate geographic expansion in key emerging markets

A set of capabilities was identified in support of those priorities. They included

- Industry-based customer focus and an ability to bundle products across divisions to meet their needs
- Product management and industry marketing, including life-cycle management, service business management, and branding

- Emerging market effectiveness in the Middle East, Russia, China, and India

- Global account management, including managing cross-border installations across the five industry groups

As we have seen, the capabilities are derived right from the strategy and serve as a set of design criteria. The current organization structure and future design options can be judged on the basis of how well they are likely to deliver these capabilities. The six design drivers help complete this analysis by calling out the benefits that various strategic grouping options provide.

At V&C, we utilized the six design drivers to assess the pros and cons of the current organization in relation to the capabilities, starting with a set of interviews with twelve executives from various parts of the business around the world. A high-level summary of that assessment is shown in Table 7.1. The structure problems were obvious in some ways: managing directors of countries, each owning their own product line, their own sales organizations, and, in some cases, their own brands, competed against other V&C divisions and subsidiaries for some of the same customers. But other issues were more complex. Some geographically based business units served multiple vertical markets, for example, whereas others were fully dedicated to a single industry. Salespeople in some geographic units were dedicated to vertical markets, but in others they were generalists who worked across industry groups. Channel strategies were not well established, and changes in sales structure could not be effective without those strategies. Product and brand management were quite fractured and would require substantial changes. After completing the assessment against the design drivers, a problem statement was crafted to summarize the case for change, as shown in Exhibit 7.1.

TABLE 7.1. *Current-State Assessment at V&C Ltd. Using the Six Design Drivers*

| Design Drivers | Benefits of Current Design | Liabilities of Current Design |
| --- | --- | --- |
| Management attention | | • Emerging markets do not receive top management attention, focus, or time. |
| Leveraged resources and cost | • Marketing communications service center provides cost-effective material development and distribution. | • We do not leverage the strengths of our best brands, globally.<br>• Local management of manufacturing has led to greatly suboptimized production capacity.<br>• There is a high degree of support staff proliferation across geographic units. |
| Coordination and integration | • Most integration occurs on a geographic basis. | • Current geographic and product orientation leads to a fractured view of the five key vertical industries.<br>• Most customers do not see the breadth and scope of our offering; it is difficult to bundle solutions.<br>• It is difficult to manage across products to serve global accounts. |
| Specialization | • Current organization provides a high degree of product specialization for sales reps. | • The current structure lacks product management roles and competence.<br>• Marketing roles are highly inconsistent across products and geographic units.<br>• Emerging market ownership is divided among current product divisions—lack of clear ownership is especially evident in China. |
| Control and accountability | • There is very clear accountability for geographic product units. | • Country manager P&L focus creates internal competition for the same customers. |
| Learning and motivation | • Geographic units create high degrees of local clarity and ownership. | • It is difficult to create general management career paths within geographic units. |

EXHIBIT 7.1. PROBLEM STATEMENT—
V&C LTD.

V&C's current organization, although successful on a regional basis, is an obstacle to leveraging the company's global reach and opportunities for growth:

- Competing geographic P&L centers cannot deliver cross-geography solutions and sometimes compete for the same business.
- Opportunities to serve global customers are being missed.
- Priorities in the factories don't always align with those of the sales units, creating delivery delays.
- Manufacturing capacity is underutilized in size and location of facilities, number of shifts, and product lines per factory.
- There is confusion about ownership and decision rights for parts of the business—for example, food and beverage in the Americas.
- The profitable service and replacement business is not given adequate attention.
- Functional depth and capability in such areas as marketing, technical sales support, industry marketing, and engineering are not given coordinated attention.

V&C leaders were now ready to begin laying out a set of alternative design concepts. We developed three strategic grouping design concepts along a continuum that ranged from less to more radical change. Diagrams to illustrate these design concepts were also developed; the preferred option is shown in Figure 7.3.

FIGURE 7.3. *Redesigned Strategic Groups for V&C Ltd. Featuring Three Vertical Market (Customer) Business Units and Horizontal Product Teams*

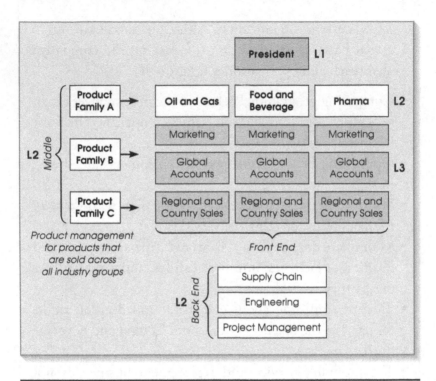

1. *Industry-focused, integrated business units with a selective matrix of horizontal product units*

Establish five vertical industry (market-based) business units, one for each of the key growth markets. These would each be led by a general manager, with its own dedicated marketing, sales, and, where possible, product management. Establish two to four horizontal product groups to manage only those product families that cannot be dedicated to a single industry leader. All other products will be managed by a vertical business unit on behalf of the larger company.

*2. Industry-focused front end with product-aligned back end*

Focus dedicated geographic sales, global accounts, and industry marketing by vertical industry, one for each of the key growth markets; reorganize back-end operations (engineering and production) into shared functional units.

*3. Product-focused (engineered and standard product groups) back end, with geography-aligned front end*

Establish a standard and an engineered product group to manage all global products, factories, service, and engineering; then dedicate sales, marketing, and service by geographic unit in newly aligned regions, with global accounts managed from the center for all industries.

For the first round of strategic grouping work, we like to generate a continuum of design options that range from radical change to something more cautious. This forces the leader and leadership team to debate the pros and cons of each and articulate their own assumptions. In this case, option 1 is the most aggressive change, clearly moving the company toward a highly customer-aligned, relatively integrated set of business units. Options 2 and 3 are both hybrids in the sense that they split the front end and the back end of the business. Option 3 represents the safest option. Products and geographic units are what V&C does well.

The design goal, illustrated in the case example, was to pull product and geographic commercial elements apart to allow global management of products, while creating more logical sets of geographic units to manage commercial, customer-facing activities. For V&C Ltd., the decision was to select option 1 as the desired strategic grouping and evolve toward it over a period of two to three years. This was, of course, only the first design decision. Building the capabilities required for this complex matrix would require new processes, linkages, decision rights, measures, and talent profiles.

# Milestone Two Summary: Strategic Grouping

*Chapter Five: Use the Six Design Drivers*

- All structures have strengths and weaknesses. An understanding of the classic building blocks of organization—function, geographic unit or region, product, and customer or market—is fundamental for generating design options.

- The six design drivers offer a helpful way to define the pros and cons of a given design option; they can be used to determine which option is most likely to help build key capabilities.

- Seek to avoid simple "either-or" choices in design; this allows you to gain, for example, the benefits of both centralized and decentralized design elements. The six design drivers can be used to help blend the benefits of multiple design options.

*Chapter Six: Choose the Best Grouping Option*

- Although there is no one right way to organize, there is usually a best choice, given the business strategy. The key is to find a solution that produces the most benefits while creating the fewest risks.

- Generate, debate, and iterate two high-level design concepts until you have selected one as the most likely to be effective.

- Once you have spelled out two or more options, they can be tested by building them out in greater detail at the next level or two down.

- Business models drive structural options. At a simple level, volume operations businesses are served better by different design options than those suitable for complex systems businesses.

- Companies today are using new criteria for setting geographic clusters, basing their decisions on their stages of market development, cultural adjacencies, external partner structures, and other factors.

- When options appear to be equally effective in addressing the design criteria, consider selecting the option that will deliver the most change over the long term, including driving necessary changes in culture when that is important to the strategy.

*Chapter Seven: Embrace the Matrix*
- The matrix organization is designed to focus management attention on two or more dimensions of the business simultaneously. It is a form of organizational complexity used to execute complex strategies.

- Tension in the matrix is evidence that competing priorities and diverse points of view are being considered.

- The most common forms of matrix structure include
  - Function versus business unit
  - Front end (geographic unit or customer) versus back end (product or function)
  - Global customer or product line versus local geographic unit

# MILESTONE
# THREE

## Integration

**MILESTONE: YOU HAVE TIED THE PIECES TOGETHER AND DEFINED POWER RELATIONSHIPS**

Once strategic grouping is complete—that is, once the framework is set for the major organizational units—it is time to begin thinking about integration. The objective is to tie the pieces back together so that work, decision making, and communication can flow horizontally as well as vertically. This is especially important for the matrix organization, as the matrix is largely about creating vigorous forms of teamwork across boundaries.

Underlying both strategic grouping and integration decisions are choices about power and complexity. Power is woven into organizations by design or through the personalities and corporate histories that mingle over time. Power is embedded vertically, in the form of authority delegated down through organizational reporting layers; it is also embedded horizontally, through decision rights and cultural norms that dictate when one business unit or department's view dominates another and when they must collaborate. In many companies, the horizontal power issues have become important to manage. At the same time, they have become more difficult for a number of reasons:

- Today's growth strategies demand that competing priorities be balanced across boundaries, especially with regard to geographic market management versus global product, brand, or category management.

- Innovation in most sectors demands greater integration of efforts across business lines, geographic units, and functions— and externally with customers and suppliers.

- Geographic footprints for business growth have shifted dramatically, and traditional regional structures are dated— often requiring the elevation of emerging markets to ensure more management attention.

- Corporate functions now demand a stronger hand in setting worldwide priorities and resource allocation for the entire function—often sparring horizontally with local and global business units.

- Pressure to reduce costs and to leverage key company resources across businesses remains high—especially when businesses must compete on cost.

The tactics for integration come in many forms and can be viewed along a spectrum developed by Galbraith (1995) and illustrated in Figure M3.1.

Mechanisms to the left represent a light touch; they encourage but do not force collaboration. Those to the right on the spectrum build in accountability for collaboration. One might assume that the process and interactive approaches, such as

FIGURE M3.1. *Methods for Creating Integration Across Strategic Groups*

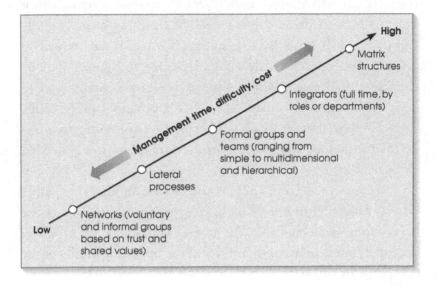

*Source:* Galbraith, 1995, p. 47

networks and councils (to the left) require more management time and that the hard-wired integrators (to the right) are automatic, and require less time. The truth is that all integration methods require management attention. When the matrix is put on "automatic" without oversight and senior leadership attention, it is likely to produce dysfunctional tension.

The options toward the left have the advantage of being more flexible and less costly than the more structural solutions to the right. These, however, still need to be deliberately designed, built, and managed to be effective. Networks and councils are well established in such companies as P&G, Nike, and Cisco, but they are not easy to institutionalize in most environments.

Cisco is an interesting case in point. The core of Cisco is a functionally oriented structure, where most employees live in engineering or sales. Leadership has been very reluctant to give up the efficiencies of this design. The cross-functional business councils, aligned around market sectors, are made up of senior executives, who invest a great deal of time in them. Initially Cisco's councils struggled to become effective. Today they drive toward a consensus on decisions that are to be executed by the functional organization. Several senior executives had to leave the business before this kind of collaboration was possible. They have become especially effective in responding to competitive situations where a cross-functional response is needed (Moore, 2005).

Of course, one company's "councils" are another company's bureaucratic nightmare. Which integrating mechanism is the best fit for a given business? The answer needs to be informed by the capabilities you want to build and the operating model of the company. In this part of the book, we

1. Introduce the *governance levers* model for designing and balancing power relationships in complex matrix organizations
2. Provide a case study of how one company deliberately and successfully used these levers to allocate and shift power from the geographic and product units to a new global category dimension in the organization
3. Illustrate how functions (HR, IT, finance, legal, marketing, and supply chain) can be designed to play more active integration roles while bringing greater value to the corporation.

# Design for Operating Governance

I NTEGRATION AND COLLABORATION ARE EXPENSIVE in terms OF management time and attention. Time spent negotiating with colleagues is time away from customers and employees. Forcing integration where it does not add value slows the company down and wastes resources. Management teams that have a clear picture of how the various units should interrelate—the operating model for the company—make decisions and move faster than those that do not. The operating model determines where and how closely organizational units need to be linked together. Just like capabilities, the operating model informs every step in the design process, as shown in Figure 8.1, but especially the Integration phase.

## OPERATING MODELS

In holding companies, decision making can be quite decentralized into the operating units, with little expectation of integration. The work of leadership in a holding company is portfolio

FIGURE 8.1. *The Operating Model for the Organization Informs Design Decisions Throughout the Design Process*

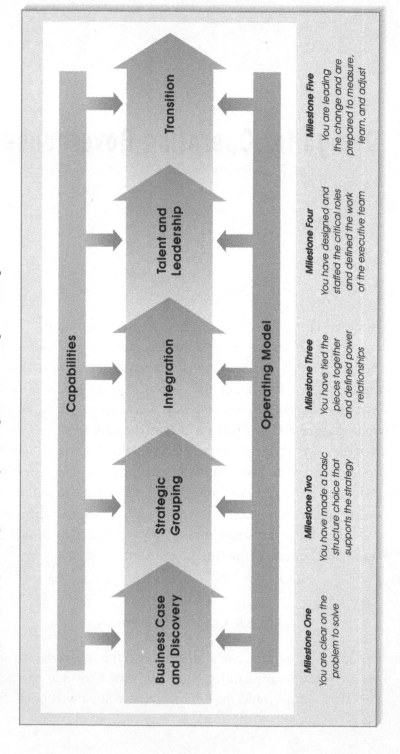

management—managing a set of assets against a financial-risk profile and an objective. It is corporate management's job to allocate capital among the business units and then to delegate how that capital is allocated within each. There is little or no need for common processes, practices, or even synergies across those businesses. Executive committees in these companies are not teams but groups, with very little interdependence. Functions are lean and have limited influence in the operating units. If there is a matrix in companies that adopt this operating model, it will be quite simple and used sparingly. The holding company typically chooses to limit integration among units in order to be able to divest assets that are not meeting prescribed financial hurdles. The more loosely coupled, the easier they are detached when they no longer fit the portfolio strategy.

In contrast, the work of management in a fully integrated, single-business company is to execute a competitive strategy—competing to win at a profit within a market. Corporate functions contribute directly to supporting operators, synergies are expected, and the executive committee needs to be a close-knit operating team. Lines of authority tend to be fairly clear in this operating model. If there is a matrix at all, it tends to be a simple one, often linking functions into geographic units.

But the two extremes—holding company and single business—do not characterize most large organizations today. Instead, most operate somewhere in between with a portfolio of related businesses that have to share common infrastructure. One operating model isn't better than another, but a model does need to be chosen. The choice then has an impact on what decisions are made about strategic grouping and integration. Table 8.1 summarizes the characteristics of the spectrum of operating models.

The integration issue is most complex for companies that manage a set of related businesses. Today's environment makes

TABLE 8.1. *Continuum View of Four Types of Company Operating Models and Their Relative Traits*

| I. Integrated (Single Business) | II. Divisional (Closely Related Portfolio) | III. Hybrid (Loosely Related Portfolio) | IV. Holding Company (Conglomerate) |
|---|---|---|---|
| • Linked strategy guides all P&L units, with minor variations.<br>• Direction comes from organizational "center."<br>• All process and practices are common.<br>• There is a single talent pool for leadership jobs.<br>• Numerous synergies are expected.<br>• Strong centralized functions are common.<br>• A strong corporate staff is established.<br>• Executive committee acts as a close-knit operating team. | • Complementary business portfolio and core strategies are created.<br>• Synergies through common processes, including pooled front-end and back-end operations, are expected.<br>• Resource allocation decisions are made by executive committee.<br>• Single-company approach to talent management is typical.<br>• Strong corporate functions support the business units with common policies where possible.<br>• Single culture and common values are established. | • Units use common approach to setting unit strategies.<br>• Few but critical processes and systems are common (for example, procurement, ecommerce).<br>• Some planned movement of talent across units is expected.<br>• Synergies are expected only through specific shared services.<br>• Value is added through corporate oversight of capital, talent, and knowledge.<br>• Corporate functions drive best practices. | • Strategy starts with financial portfolio.<br>• Business units return financials to parent.<br>• No common processes are expected.<br>• Movement of talent across units is rare.<br>• No synergies are expected.<br>• Multiple cultures remain.<br>• Corporate staff is small and focused on fiduciary role. |
| • Simple or no matrix | • Complex matrix | • Moderate matrix | • Simple or no matrix |

the integration question more difficult still. Market turbulence requires greater organizational agility (Sull, 2009). One critical form of agility is portfolio agility, the ability to quickly shift capital and human resources asymmetrically from one business, category, or product to another. The more autonomous the business units are and the more power is delegated to them, the more difficult it is to realign investment priorities among the businesses. When general manager positions are filled with strong, seasoned leaders, senior executives at corporate become reluctant to interfere with their decisions or to make hard choices about which segment to starve and which to feed. This "equality" among businesses becomes especially detrimental to innovation investments (Moore, 2005). The allocation of power and resources is the work of corporate leadership. These decisions are made not only at the highest levels of the firm but also at multiple levels into regions and business units.

*Operating governance* is how managers within a business delegate decision making *vertically* into the organization through hierarchy, policy, and controls and establish decision rights *horizontally* across functions and business units. Operating governance is the process—through design or happenstance—by which power is allocated. Power allocation through governance is core to organization design.

As a practical matter, operating governance is the sorting of decision rights among roles. It shapes the interactions between global and local units, between center-led functions and operating divisions, and even between internal groups and external partners.

A clear approach to operating governance is the key to making the tension in the matrix work for customers, owners, and employees in business. Table 8.2 lists examples of the potential areas of tension between global product and geographic general managers.

TABLE 8.2. *Typical Power Struggles Between Global and Local Geographic Units*

| Global Product Division | Local Geographic Management |
|---|---|
| Center sets product investment priorities—new technology (fewer, bigger bets). | Countries expect strong voice in product creation priorities—and often continue to fund local innovations. |
| Global product standards, specs, and pricing corridors are set as policy. | Local units seek to adapt product to local customer or consumer needs and expect latitude in tactical pricing. |
| Center ensures that all aspects of brand management are aligned with positioning. | Countries want brand "stories" to be relevant to local consumers. |
| Center provides best practices and guidelines for developing local media strategies. | Countries press for locally relevant media strategies, and manage execution. |
| Center provides global copy strategy for major advertising initiatives. | Countries tailor global campaigns to maximize impact. |
| Center sets demand-creation budget for global. | Regions set demand-creation budget for the geographic units. |

## GOVERNANCE LEVERS

Using a matrix to integrate the multiple dimensions of an organization creates complex power dynamics, requiring a high degree of management attention. Leaders continually face too many opportunities and risks and have too few resources. Limited management attention is a fundamental constraint in business execution. Just as equity, assets, and investment capital should be used judiciously to ensure an appropriate return, so to should the scarce and expensive resource of management time and attention (Simons, 1995). When power dynamics in the complex organization are not designed well, the result is prolonged decision making, misunderstood communication, and friction caused by competing priorities. Positive return on management comes from orchestrating the natural tensions efficiently in the best interest of customers, employees, and owners.

A number of tools have been developed to clarify roles and responsibilities, beginning with Schein's development of RACI charting that clarifies who is responsible and accountable for a decision, who must be consulted, and who must be informed (Schein, 2004). RACI has been recently updated to RAPID—recommend, agree, perform, input, decision—with the same goal of clearly identifying who has decision authority (Rogers and Blenko, 2006).

Many managers and organization development professionals are well versed in using these decision tools, which are quite effective for mapping straightforward decisions within a process. Once decisions become more complex and therefore require collaboration rather than delegation, and nuanced trade-offs rather than application of simple criteria, these tools are less effective on their own. They are far more likely to gain traction when they are part of a systemic and behavioral view of operating governance—when there is a framework that defines power relationships, boundaries, points of control, and the beliefs that people share about running the business.

We have adapted Simons's levers-of-control model (1995, 2005) into a framework for the design of power dynamics of complex, multidimensional organizations. The model serves as a way for leaders to consciously make governance part of strategy execution and provides the framework in which decision rights tools can be used effectively.

The four levers of control are used to energize and channel resources in relation to a business strategy (Simons, 1995). In Simons's original work, these levers of strategy execution are defined as

1. *Belief systems,* used to inspire and direct the search for new opportunities

2. *Interactive networks,* used to stimulate organizational learning and the emergence of new ideas and strategies

3. *Boundary systems,* used to set limits on opportunity-seeking behavior

4. *Diagnostic control systems,* used to monitor and reward achievement of specified goals

The four levers are grouped into two opposing forces—the yin and yang—of effective strategy implementation. Two of these control levers—belief systems and interactive networks—create positive and inspirational forces. They drive innovative thinking. The other two levers—boundary systems and diagnostic control systems—create constraints and ensure compliance, thereby focusing managerial attention away from activities that are distracting or not central to the strategy. The model is shown in Figure 8.2.

FIGURE 8.2. *The Four Levers of Control*

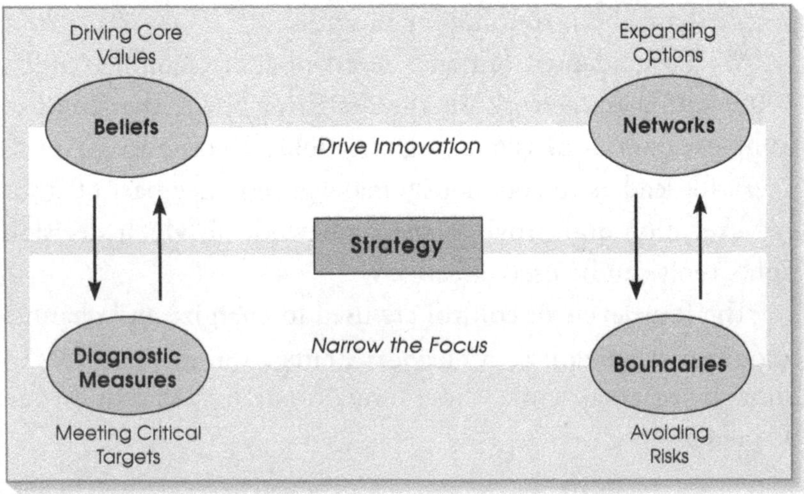

*Source:* Adapted from Simons, 2005

An optimal return on management is achieved by creating a proper balance between these competing levers and providing effective decision rules. We believe that governing the matrix means finding the balance in these forces (Kesler and Schuster, 2009). Underpowering or overcontrolling a key axis in the matrix destroys initiative, creativity, and value. Unlimited freedom granted to all axes in the matrix results in lack of focus, poor return on management, and weak execution.

### Governance of the Matrix

The four *governance levers*, as we have chosen to call them for our purposes, help bring the matrix to life by orchestrating healthy tension among the roles. The levers employ the full spectrum of integration mechanisms—networks, linking processes, teams, and integrative roles—to support the matrix. Figure 8.3 spells out a set of action items that we have found useful in relation to each of the four levers. The objective is to establish the right mix of tactics to support the capabilities we seek. Each lever is discussed in detail in the next sections.

*Beliefs.*    Beliefs are an explicit set of organizational norms that senior managers communicate and reinforce in order to provide values, purpose, and direction to the organization. Beliefs inspire the search for opportunities to increase value, and guide managers on the expectations for managing relationships internally and externally.

Beliefs are most likely to be effective in companies that have strong cultures and leadership norms. A well-defined vision for the business produces shared beliefs. For example, P&G's CEO, A. G. Lafley, was very successful in creating a common understanding that the company improves the lives of people in developed and emerging markets with its health, beauty, and

FIGURE 8.3. *Sampling of Effective Tactics for Balancing Power (Using Each of the Four Governance Levers)*

| | Drive Innovation | |
|---|---|---|
| **Beliefs** | • Company vision and values<br>• Direct management interaction<br>• Customer visits<br>• Internal education programs | • Corporate social responsibility commitments<br>• Executive speeches and blogs |
| **Networks** | • Global business planning teams<br>• Executive talent reviews<br>• Talent movement<br>• Colocation arrangements | • Formal networks and councils<br>• Distributor and partner forums<br>• Action-learning teams<br>• Ideation teams |
| | Create Focus | |
| **Boundaries** | • Decision rights docs<br>• Role definition<br>• Formal business process<br>• Product standards and control | • HR policy and practices<br>• Brand policy<br>• Procurement policy |
| **Diagnostic Measures** | • Business dashboards<br>• Cascaded objectives<br>• Business reviews<br>• Individual performance management | • Internal and external benchmarking<br>• Audits |

home care products. These core values create common purpose to integrate the energies of widely dispersed category, geographic, and functional leaders who must work within a matrix to bring global brands to local markets.

Here is a set of action items and tools used by companies that have built a strong foundation of shared beliefs:

- *Company vision and values.* Most employees are deeply interested in the vision of the business and want to be part of companies that have a clear sense of direction and commitment to values. Credibility comes through visible leadership role models that embody the written statements.

- *Direct management interaction.* The more that people interact directly with senior leaders to work through challenges and conflict, the greater the alignment in beliefs. It is impressive to watch executives in our client companies who are very actively involved in sorting through cross-boundary problems; direct interaction is the best opportunity to role-model collaborative ways of working.

- *Customer visits.* Customer visits are opportunities to role-model the right norms. At Coca-Cola, for example, when executives visit local markets, they walk the streets in Bangkok, Mexico City, Madrid, and New York with local sales and franchise people to talk to the owners of small outlets as well as to major retailers.

- *Internal education programs.* These are an opportunity to teach the strategy of the business and the role of organization in execution, as well as to impart key philosophies that drive decision making. Intel provides training on how to manage conflict in the matrix, and requires all new hires to participate.

- *Corporate social responsibility (CSR) commitments.* CRS helps maintain an external point of view and increasingly serves as a shared focal point for teams around the world; cross-functional teams often work on initiatives in far-off locations. The experience not only solves specific issues but also can lead to greater identity with the values of the company.

- *Executive speeches and blogs.* Executives deliver key messages to internal and external audiences that can be used to align expectations across the management team. Many executives now routinely blog with the workforce, helping build common understanding on complex issues affecting the company.

*Networks.*   Exploiting market opportunities requires organizations to break out of limited search routines. Networks are the catalyst for innovation and adaptation. Well-designed networks allow people to work across nodes to scan the environment and share information and insights. One of the purposes of a matrix organization is to promote creativity by bringing divergent points of view into contact. People come together to challenge each other, debate options, and develop ideas that might never emerge inside a stand-alone business unit.

Interactive governance practices are likely to be easier in companies with rich traditions of dialogue and relationship building. Bartlett and Ghoshal (1989) argued for the importance of relationships and other "soft" processes as means of building matrix effectiveness across organizational and national borders. Integration tactics are cumulative. One must be adept at building and managing networks and teams before moving toward multidimensional matrix forms.

Antonio Lucio, former chief marketing officer at PepsiCo, outlined an example of interactive governance at work in the brand giant. His goal was to make local marketers and bottlers successful. Lucio (2008) explains:

> *We operate through a bottom-up, highly participatory and interactive process. It is lengthy and time-consuming, but highly effective. There is a committee—consisting of people from the top 29 countries around the world—that drives everything we do. At Pepsi, the local marketer owns the branding locally: the actual manifestation of the positioning statement within the context of his/her particular market. What we, at the center, do is to provide a menu of programs,*

*that first and foremost, those local guys helped develop. They provide
input to everything we do at the center and at each and every step of
the development process—from advertising to product development.*

Here are some practices for building effective networks:

• *Global business planning teams.* Assign players from around
the world to update strategic plans or complete new product
planning before setting investment plans to build ownership;
bring customers and outside experts into the process to expand
thinking.

• *Executive talent reviews and talent movement.* Make it clear
to the organization that global thinkers and people willing to
move laterally to other businesses and functions will be show-
cased and will be promoted to key positions. To shift power in
the matrix, load up one axis or another with stronger leaders.

• *Colocation arrangements.* Create close working connections by arranging work spaces so that people who should be
interacting regularly will do so without regard to reporting relationships; place centers of expertise out in the field, near the
internal clients.

• *Formal networks and councils.* Establish standing, cross-
divisional councils around key customers, platform technologies, brands, or critical functions that lack a corporate power
center. Zara, the Spanish fashion giant, has been very successful
with standing, cross-functional design teams who are in constant contact with local markets. These networks can work quite
effectively in nearly all cultures to govern across nations and
functions.

• *Distributor and external partner forums.* Many companies
maintain formal and informal interactive forums with distribution and other external partners to build linkages. These

relationships not only cement collaboration outside but also reinforce beliefs internally.

• *Action-learning teams.* Take learning teams to emerging market locations and expose them to diverse external thinkers, customers, and challenges. Engage senior executives from different axes in the matrix, and ask them to work together to select the best ideas for implementation.

• *Ideation teams.* Conduct new product ideation with diverse collections of people from around the world, and make certain that the people who can act on those ideas are part of the process.

*Boundaries.*   Boundaries are where most governance efforts focus, specifying policy, rules, and decision guardrails that must be used. Boundaries should not be considered a negative or limiting aspect of governance. As Simons points out, the purpose of brakes on a car is not to slow it down but to allow the driver to go fast (Simons, 1995). Clear parameters create a well-defined space that permits freedom and channels creativity. Clarity of strategy, trade-offs, and decision criteria speed decision making by avoiding the need to escalate conflicts upward.

Strategic boundaries place limits on what opportunities may be pursued in the search for growth and innovation in order to preserve value. For example, at Nike, it's *not* okay for locally generated product enhancements to diminish or contradict the brand stories that come from the center. At Colgate, the geographic business units are empowered to adapt products to local habits and tastes, but the brand book for Colgate's red toothpaste icon makes it very clear how the brand will be positioned and that the brand boundaries must not be violated.

The following are examples of practices that create integrating boundaries for large companies. Many of these exist in most companies but are not formalized or applied as consistently as they need to be to create clarity rather than conflict or confusion:

- *Decision rights.* Leaders across the business should be taught to use RACI and RAPID tools to work through the key decision points that will be faced once the new organization is implemented. These tools are useful only when they are pressure tested in difficult business situations. They are living documents that should be reworked periodically.

- *Role definition.* It is important to spell out responsibilities, metrics, and selection criteria for all key positions in a new organization design; these should be drafted at one time, as an integrated set of roles. John Deere has an established practice of posting management role definitions on internal sites intended to increase shared understanding of people's work and priorities.

- *Formal business process.* Decision rights make more sense when they are tied to a business process map, something tangible that defines the major steps in the work. For example, separate product groups can operate with significant degrees of freedom as long as a common go-to-market process links them at the customer interface. Figure 8.4 illustrates the concept-to-store process used by a retailer.

- *Product standards and controls.* In businesses that rely on a common systems architecture, separate units can create modules to satisfy specific customer needs, as long as a common set of standards ensures integration.

- *Human resources policy and practice.* Companies like GE have required for decades that the staffing of all positions at a given level be coordinated by a center-based control point for

FIGURE 8.4. *A Go-to-Market Process for a Large Fashion Retailer Shows Decision Points in the Business Process*

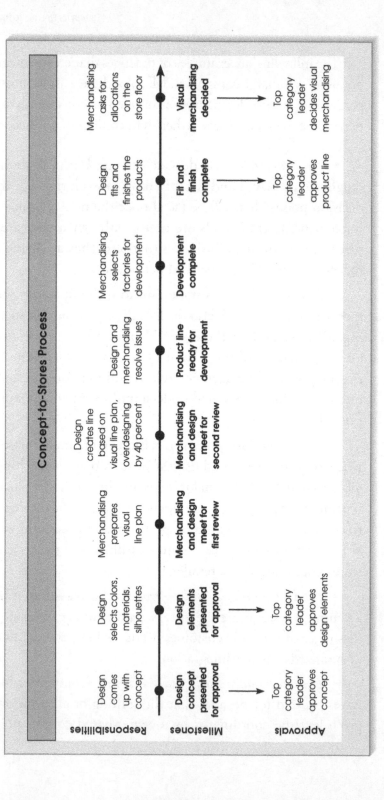

candidate slates. This ensures that an enterprise-wide view is taken into account. These and many other HR practices can be highly effective at integrating units and making it easier for people to work together across boundaries.

- *Brand policy.* Many companies that have built a house-of-brands organization delegate degrees of autonomy to product management groups, but insist that brand assets are managed strategically from the center.

- *Procurement policy and process.* Even highly decentralized product divisions must often cooperate with center-led procurement practices to ensure that the corporation is leveraging its size and power with vendors and suppliers for high-value purchasing.

*Diagnostic Measures.*    Diagnostic tools monitor results and behavior in relation to the strategies, objectives, and fiduciary accountabilities of a company. These are the measures that drive the right behaviors in the business and allow *self-correction.* Diagnostics include classic financial controls (such as the income statement and balance sheet) as well as process-focused measures and customer measures used to build capability. Measurement-based governing methods have been drivers of innovation in companies that have established dominance in a particular competence, such as Walmart (supplier management), Dell (cash and inventory management), and 3M (new product creation).

Leaders should work with data to assess trends and risks, and make tough decisions. It is now clear that the meltdown of capital markets in 2008 was related to a shortage of diagnostic controls as well as a lack of management understanding of the risks that were being incurred in opaque derivatives and the collateralized debt beneath them. The matrix organization in institutions like Citigroup (organized around three axes: customers, geography, and products) had become quite complex. Despite continuous efforts to integrate the units at Citicorp, its top executives appeared unable to manage the power struggles within the matrix.

The most powerful and integrating diagnostic controls in the matrix are those that force dialogue and problem solving across boundaries:

• *Business dashboards.* Metrics are a key element of the Star Model; for the business to succeed, accountabilities need to be balanced and aligned among positions that work together. P&L alignments should be carefully considered to ensure that the greater good of the business is not compromised by each profit center's optimizing its own success.

• *Reporting systems.* Information is power. Information management systems that make data and performance easily accessible and transparent increase insight into the impact of local decisions on enterprise performance.

• *Cascaded objectives.* One of the most powerful integrators is aligned objectives that have been worked vertically and horizontally throughout the organization; this process should be tied to networks and councils to maximize the contracting and alignment among units.

• *Business reviews.* Team-based business reviews that blend membership from geographic units, global product units, and functions are another logical practice. Teams put diagnostics to use through dialogue and problem solving, attack gaps jointly, and test and debate decision rights in the context of difficult problems.

• *Individual performance management.* Business reviews should be translated into individual performance reviews throughout the business. In the matrix, everyone has two bosses who must collaborate on setting goals and managing performance. Some companies designate one axis in the matrix as having a stronger vote in the final rating or have the managers evaluate different aspects of performance. This collaborative approach should extend to defining the potential of individual leaders. The importance of these integrating practices cannot be overemphasized as a way to align behaviors in the matrix.

• *Benchmarking practices and audits.* Both internal and external benchmarks are useful for creating discomfort that prods diagnostic thinking. Companies like P&G and Nestlé that have made the matrix a way of life for decades insist that managers spend time doing "search and reapply" with their teams in other parts of the globe; Coke marketers in North Africa study the successful practices of their colleagues in Latin America to find ideas to bring back and reapply.

### When to Work the Levers

The chosen levers should be outlined during the Integration phase of an organization project. They can be adjusted, eliminated, and renewed at any time in order to maintain and enhance organization effectiveness. Problems in business execution can often be directly linked to failures in the governance process. Here are some examples of execution problems that may indicate it is time to adopt new levers and tactics:

• *Key customer issues*—lost sales or confusion in handling key account decisions

• *Failed new product launches*—poor sales results, missed deadlines, or reliability problems

- *Repeated false starts in key emerging markets*—failed efforts to establish critical mass in an important geographic market

- *Difficulties developing new selling channels in the legacy business*—new business practices stamped out by old ones

- *Lack of executives with international experience*—overreliance on host-country ex-pats, failures in making cross-national moves, or a lack of leadership-replacement talent

- *Cost issues*—more resources added with each new initiative, none removed; lower margins than those of competitors

# Allocate Power in the Matrix

## A Case Study in Governance

THE OBJECTIVE IN APPLYING THE GOVERNANCE levers is to find the right mix to support the capabilities you seek. The story of Apparel Brands Inc. (ABI; although this is a real company, the name has been changed) offers valuable insights into how the framework can be used.

ABI is a highly successful $10 billion marketer of apparel and accessory brands. Its brands are very visible all over the world, and its quality products enjoy attractive margins as a result of the power of those brands. The organization had strong product-focused business units, matrixed with geographic divisions. The structure had served the company well for more than a decade. But ABI began to discover that its intense focus on great product was limiting its ability to communicate directly with consumers, and the relative autonomy of its geographic regions had made delivering compelling brand stories around the world more difficult.

ABI leadership had set an aggressive growth target to double the size of the business in five years. The intention was to accomplish this through better alignment of the organization with highly dynamic consumer segments. The result was a strategic decision to develop, market, and manage through global, consumer-focused categories rather than products. Categories are different from products at ABI; they are market segments that reflect a very consumer-centric view. Brand marketers worked with top executives at ABI to define five lifestyle-oriented consumer segments: urban, indie, sports, metro, and outdoor. The vision was to create a powerful franchise of consumer communities on a global scale. An overarching brand story would integrate them, but each would be empowered to develop apparel collections that appealed to its target consumer. This meant forcing a new consumer view across the traditional product lines of tops, bottoms, footwear, and accessories.

In defining consumer-centric capabilities for the new category strategy, it became clear that the old structure made it difficult to build consumer-aligned categories because the product units each went to market separately and on different seasonal calendars. Products that the outdoor consumer might naturally buy together in a collection would arrive weeks apart or fail to complement in fabric and color. And it was very difficult to launch big, global ideas because the regional geographic units still set their own seasonal priorities.

It was clear to ABI's leaders that the new consumer-focused strategy called for less geographic autonomy and less focus on product, and more global consumer category voice in the operating governance of the company. Top executives spelled out a set of organization design criteria. They sought an organization that would

- Create and sustain relationships by consumer segments, and drive all decision making through a consumer lens
- Deliver great consumer experiences—product, services, and content

- Enable category-focused collections to arrive in each market according to a synched seasonal calendar
- Reach the point where 50 percent of SKUs in local assortments are drawn from global assortments

These criteria led to a strategic grouping decision to realign the product business units into five global, consumer-aligned category business units, and to refocus the product business units into smaller, product development functions. A new corporate design function, closely linked to brand marketing, would bring more creative excellence (through specialization) to the mix. Figures 9.1 and 9.2 illustrate the old and the new structures.

FIGURE 9.1. *ABI's Legacy Product- and Geography-Based Matrix*

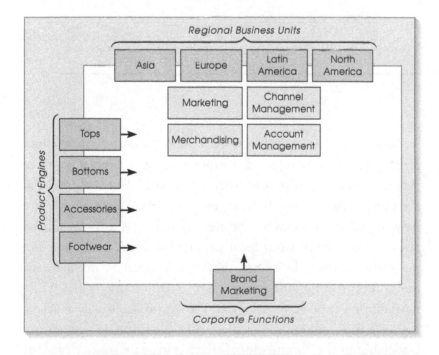

FIGURE 9.2. *ABI's New Organization Design Focused on Consumer Categories*

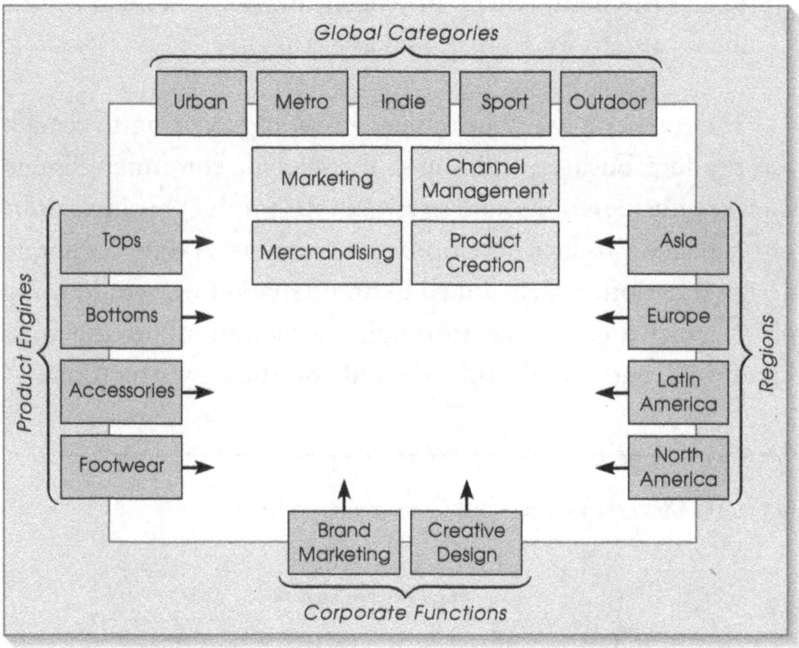

Matrix tension is nothing new to ABI, and cynicism had long ago given way to gentle humor among insiders who agree that a matrix is "just part of working at ABI." But the potential for confusion and bottlenecks was ratcheted higher with the new organization launch. The new global categories would be taking power both from local geographic units and from the powerful product divisions. They would need to do so without compromising local relevance in critical markets and while maintaining product excellence. The corporate brand marketing organization would be expected to continue its very strong leadership of the "brand ethos." Even with a persuasive case for change and cooperation from a broad base of leadership, the operating governance challenges were significant.

Shortly after the announcement of the new organization, a steering committee composed of the COO and his direct reports set about actively managing the transition. Subteams, guided by the steering committee, were assigned to complete several parallel work streams at the start—all aimed at effective completion of what the COO described as the most difficult change ever initiated in the company. The four governance levers were used as a framework for guiding the change strategy.

Among the various work streams was a process-design team charged with defining a common go-to-market process that would be used by all categories to ensure a coordinated approach each season. Process designers were flummoxed by the difficulties in defining who had decision authority at each of the key junctures in the process. Such decisions as locking in global product designs, setting global product assortments, and planning worldwide launches and ad campaigns were not simple ones that could be easily mapped out in a RACI or RAPID grid. The challenge would be to manage the tension among categories, geographic units, and several functions through each go-to-market phase in a manner that served consumers, and ultimately shareholders, in the best way possible.

## THE BELIEFS LEVER AT ABI

Beliefs should drive the search for opportunities. ABI has made its values statement part of the management process for years. But the executive steering committee reached beyond company values to guide the implementation of the new category structure at ABI. A compelling business case was the starting point. The CEO and COO worked together to create a leadership document that laid out the exciting trends under way within the five different consumer communities that were at the core of ABI's opportunities. Shifts among competitors were described along with larger business forces—all adding up to a persuasive case for change. The road show went external and internal and was very much focused on shaping beliefs about the future growth prospects for the company. The message to the shareholders was no different than the message to the internal audience. The passion of the executive team was real, and the business case was crafted with real consumer insight and global market data.

Confidence in the brand is a core belief at ABI, as it is in many great brand companies. Executive leadership was quite effective at ABI in leveraging that confidence to rally the organization around the power of the brand to deliver very aggressive growth in the new flying formation.

Teamwork is another core belief at ABI. Executives understood that it would be very difficult to maintain the collaborative culture while signaling a shift in power to a new group of general managers running the new category business units, who were expected to act more quickly and decisively than the product units had in the past. The COO was determined to maximize his own time spent out in the organization coaching geographic teams through the transition. His own long tenure in the company made him a credible voice for the new approach to governance.

## Interactive Networks at ABI

Interactive networks are central to organizational learning. They allow leaders to consider prospective changes in the market and in the economy, and they alert key actors to the changing future needs of the business. They create dialogue within the organization that produces revisions to the strategy and, subsequently, the other three governance levers.

At ABI, colocation of team members was key to the organizing principles of the category teams. Although most of the functional actors in each category remained strongly tethered back to functional centers, they were colocated with their category counterparts in large warehouse-like spaces with lots of color and light. There were few walls in these spaces (except for those used for displaying drawings and ideas), and designers, marketers, developers, and financial people interacted constantly. They frequently welcomed outside guests—consumers who represented their target market—into the workspace.

The new organization required councils that were more formal than had been used in the past. Merchandising was one of the critical skill sets that had to be enhanced across the company, but there was reluctance to establish another corporate function. Instead, merchandisers across the categories and product units formed a council with clear objectives for redefining roles and critical competencies, retraining current staff, and actively recruiting stronger talent into the function.

Few governance practices have more impact than interactive talent reviews. The chief human resources officer at ABI worked to create a strong role for the corporate center in facilitating worldwide talent forums. The new approach tipped the matrix away from product and geography to a stronger functional and category voice in how leaders were evaluated, including a "51 percent vote" in staffing and promotion decisions across the company. The new process required open dialogue. Functional, category, and regional leaders compared and debated their assessments of shared talent. Talent decisions were played out in these forums at least two levels deep into the organization. After two annual cycles, the change in behavior can be startling, and ABI was no exception.

Interactive business planning was another powerful lever for governing decisions at ABI. Product- and geography-focused strategic planning was replaced in the first full year of the new organization with a category-focused strategy lens. Initial strategy meetings were awkward. Product and regional leaders bit their tongues when category general managers brought their business cases forward. But the learning was quick, and soon category strategies were translated into annual and quarterly go-to-market plans.

Worldwide leadership met to decide what the apparel collections would look like three or more seasons ahead. European managers balked at the thought that American-based leaders could make fashion choices that would suit European consumers. But highly interactive governance processes ensured the input of strong, consumer-focused voices from many parts of the world in those decisions. Mistakes were made. In some categories, the global center overreached its ability to create "global product." In others, assertive geographic managers dragged the process backward. But adjustments were made in the second cycle, people listened, and the results were favorable.

One of the major conclusions after the second cycle of go-to-market planning was that the process was too burdensome, required too many people in the room at one time, and was simply too expensive to operate. More efficient practices for gaining input and ownership had to be considered. In retrospect, however, overinvolvement at the start was a necessary step for building trust. After a few rounds, people began to trust others to act on their behalf. As a result, fewer people were needed to effectively participate in some decision-making forums, and decision making was streamlined.

## BOUNDARIES AT ABI

Boundaries impose limits on teams' and individuals' search for opportunities. Brand is the heartbeat at ABI, and it is the inspiration for much creativity. But there are also controls intended to avoid brand-diminishing decisions and behaviors inside the company and with its franchise and retail partners.

In the matrix, the supply chain function had not traditionally had a strong leadership presence in the company. But in the emergent category structure, its role needed to be strengthened in order to improve the economics of the procurement spend—an increasingly important element of strategy alignment. In a horizontal rebalancing of power, the supply chain function was further centralized and granted decision rights in the go-to-market process.

After roles were clearly defined for each axis in the matrix (over an eighteen-month period), the steering committee developed a set of decision rights for the go-to-market process, spelling out who owned the decisions for several key decision points. These were worked widely across the company, with edits along the way, until every function and business unit had put its imprint somewhere on the documents. Two years later, a second round of reviews led to more edits, based on two years of experience in the new category organization. Table 9.1 shows a sample of the decision rights work for category marketing.

## DIAGNOSTIC MEASURES AT ABI

ABI did not have a strong history of effective measurement, but the new global category GM roles had to be measured effectively relative to other senior leaders in the business. Steering committee members laid out measures for all key roles side by side. The categories were given clear market measures to establish

TABLE 9.1. *A Portion of ABI's Decision Rights Matrix*

| | Role | | | |
|---|---|---|---|---|
| Decision | Category | Product Engine | Geography | Brand Marketing |
| Set design ethos for category | D | | I | R |
| Design product, decide specific features | R | D | I | |
| Write product briefs | I | D | P | R |
| Select color and materials | D | R | I | |
| Set aligned product creation calendar | R | D | P | |
| Manage product creation stage gates | P | | | |
| Measure innovation performance | D | I | I | R |

R = Recommend  A = Agree  P = Perform  I = Input  D = Decide

their ownership for the consumer. Profitability was defined as gross margin, based on the ability of categories to set prices and drive revenues through superior product innovations and brand strategies. Regional general managers were assigned operating income metrics based on their ability to sell to retail accounts and influence retail sell-through to consumers. Regions carried allocated corporate costs as well, given that they continued to own the most assets and people in the business. Realigning the reporting systems was a challenge, requiring two years of manual reporting during the transition. Robust performance reviews and other management routines were established to work through the results on a continual basis.

ABI management maintained attention to setting, adjusting, and readjusting the levers over a three-year period of time following the initial organization redesign. Figure 9.3 summarizes how the governance levers model was applied at ABI.

The ABI case offers these lessons:

1. The four governance levers must be aligned and integrated into a whole to be effective in creating the optimal balance of vertical and horizontal power across units. Any decision rules created then need to reflect the desired balance.
2. By nature, some organizational units (for example, product development) tend to act as catalysts for divergence and innovation, whereas others (for example, finance) are charged with constraining opportunities and focusing attention. These realities should be considered in balancing the formal power that each is given in the matrix.
3. Each of the four levers will be more or less useful in a given culture. Attention should be given to whether goals are best served by introducing practices that are culture-friendly or by selecting practices to challenge the culture. Both are likely to be appropriate, but should be considered deliberately.
4. Openness to new ideas was easy in the ABI culture. More hidebound companies find this difficult. Setting the right interactive practices is critical to keeping leadership tied to the outside forces that matter. Controls are important, but governance must also serve to keep the business open to new ideas.
5. The cost of management time in an effective matrix is higher than in simple structures. Complexity, decision delay, frustration over time spent on internal negotiations, and gaps in decision quality can be vexing. Thus, in

FIGURE 9.3. *Governance Levers Used to Rebalance Power in the Matrix at ABI*

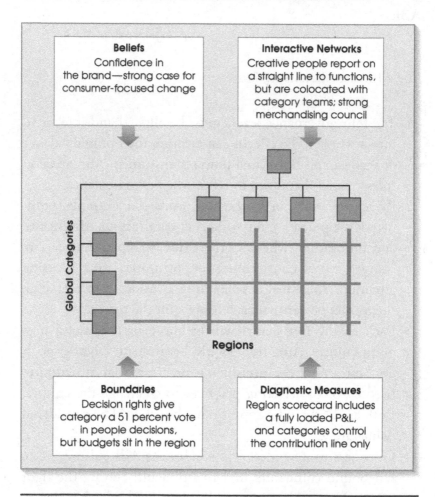

looking at decision rules and operating governance frameworks, management needs to be guided not by architectural elegance but rather by return on management time and expense. Does giving more people more input improve the quality of decision making, or does it strangle initiative in endless process?

# Redesign Functions to Be Integrators

FUNCTIONS (INCLUDING HR, FINANCE, IT, LEGAL, MARKETING, AND SUPPLY CHAIN) can serve as the mortar that holds the building blocks of a closely related portfolio of businesses together. The HR organization integrates the operating units by delivering common approaches to selecting people, by creating alignment with the right rewards systems, and by stewarding leadership talent as a company-wide asset that can be redeployed across businesses. Finance integrates the business operating units by driving common measurement systems, setting financial targets, and helping ensure that capital moves to the right opportunities in the portfolio. Corporate IT, legal, and supply chain functions all play similar roles in holding the separate organizational building blocks together. The more there is opportunity to gain benefits from synergy between business units, the greater the opportunity for functions to serve as integrators.

## THE "PROBLEM WITH CORPORATE"

Today's corporate-center functions often struggle to define the distinct value they add to the growth agenda for the business. In many companies, corporate staffs suffer identity crises, and the top talent is drawn to big jobs in the operating units rather than to roles in the center. For example, division presidents often love their own HR partners but rate the competence of the overall function consistently low, and are constantly battling to reduce allocated costs from the center. Conflicts over roles and decision rights become commonplace, staffers are frustrated with their ability to have impact, and successive rounds of cost reduction continue to reduce capability indiscriminately. This dynamic repeats itself between the corporate level and the divisions and from the division or regional level down to the local units.

Companies that make the most progress in designing effective finance, HR, and IT functions create tight focus on how and where work is generated. They view the functions not just as compliance or service entities but as important information conduits and horizontal integrators. The ability of the functions to bring the right information forward enables better business decision making (Boudreau and Ramstad, 2007).

These companies have taken up the challenge to design the function from "end to end." This means examining all activity and resources in the function at the center, across geographic units, and across business units as a collective in order to reconsider the overall cost and impact the function has on the business. The challenge starts with visibility. In many organizations, it is difficult even to identify how many people are doing finance work around the world.

In end-to-end function design, the value framework is converted into a delivery model and then an organization structure. The "center" and the "field" are designed as one integrated capability, with separate but linked roles to play. The human resources organization is a good example to illustrate the benefits of an end-to-end view of function design, but this analysis applies to any support function. In the traditional approach, "global" responsibility is assigned to the center, which manages an overarching HR strategy and a well-defined set of corporate HR activities and resources for the greater interest of the enterprise. In this model, the regional and business HR teams are closely aligned with the business leaders. Their costs are budgeted by the businesses, and they have considerable leeway in practices and in staffing their own functions. In many companies, they customize corporate initiatives to fit local needs. This popular model is expected to create an effective "strategic business partner." Business leaders with a competent partner are generally satisfied with their local support. However, the model misses the opportunity to leverage the function as an integrative device for the enterprise. Typically, one finds

- Limited consistency in core HR processes, deliverables, and impact on the business
- Wide variation in HR skills and talent
- Higher total HR costs, due to proliferation of functional resources and often redundancy across units
- Limited information and best practice sharing or talent movement across the operating units

The end-to-end model, in contrast, establishes global HR responsibility for the entire function. Local HR resources usually continue to report to business leaders, but with strong accountability back to the center or with matrix reporting. The result is lower overall cost—though costs in the center go up—and a consistent approach to core practices. Perhaps more important, the potential to automate services is substantially better; and with redesigned processes, service delivery can be greatly improved across the company.

Of course, as with any structure, there are trade-offs. In the end-to-end model, the risk is lack of responsiveness from the center. As power is shifted to the center with the mandate to integrate and create consistency where variation doesn't add value, the center tends to dictate. Rather than enabling the business units, the center becomes a bottleneck, slowing decision making and constraining ideas and innovation. The cause of this predictable and negative consequence of shifting power is a lack of clarity regarding the role of the center. Merely defining a split between center and field is too simplistic. In fact, the "center" does not have to refer to work and people who sit in the corporate offices at all. Companies are becoming more creative about leaving centers of know-how out in the geographic units, where they remain close to the businesses, customers, and employees. This helps reframe the centralized versus decentralized controversy into a more useful discussion.

The center plays three distinct roles in a function. When articulated clearly and then staffed appropriately, the center becomes an enabler of strategy rather than the ill-regarded overhead it has too often become.

## THE VALUE DELIVERY FRAMEWORK FOR THE CORPORATE CENTER

The center-led portion of a function can be designed around a three-box value delivery framework that helps ensure the best integration benefits. The three distinct roles in the framework are

1. Function oversight and strategy
2. Thought leadership
3. Selected services

FIGURE 10.1. *Value Delivery Framework for Functions in the Corporate Center*

| | Function Oversight and Strategy | Thought Leadership | Selected Services |
|---|---|---|---|
| **Key Activities** | • Strategy, policy<br>• Global standards, stewardship of key priorities in the strategy<br>• Fiduciary controls | • Center of expertise<br>• Best practices and measurement<br>• Develop priority capabilities<br>• Consultants to divisions | • Guide optimal service solutions (central, field-based, virtual, outsourced)<br>• Execute all service commitments |
| **Rationale** | • Basis of global strategy and approach to growth<br>• Common process<br>• Economies of scale | • Expertise that is difficult or expensive to replicate<br>• Best ideas attract division users<br>• Ensure focus on most critical capabilities<br>• Help build one culture | • Selective basis only:<br>  Supporting global brands, customers, projects<br>  Substantial economies available<br>• Best alternative sought: central, field-based, outsourced |
| **"Rule"** | Mandatory | By request | Mandatory participation once agreed to with divisions |

All support-function work should fit into one of the three buckets and should meet the "rules" that accompany that work. Work that does not fit into one of the three is a candidate for elimination. Figure 10.1 summarizes these roles and rules.

### *Function Oversight and Strategy*

This is the work of the top functional executive and a small group of team members. It is policy work and requires a level of authority to achieve compliance, where necessary, suited to the governance model of the corporation. This role of the function is to create strategies that solve vexing problems. In finance, these might be how the company will manage debt and equity, manage currency fluctuations, or fund strategic initiatives. In human resources, it means how to source and reward the right talent, shape culture, develop future leaders, and manage employment costs. The outputs should be few and robust, linked to the business model of the company, and appropriate to its size and geographic complexity.

The oversight role is most effective when focused on creating the criteria and guidelines for decisions and educating the business units on how to make good strategic choices. Too often, the oversight role is defined as making and signing off on decisions. This only serves to disempower the business unit, obfuscate accountability, and slow the speed of decision making.

The "rule" here is straightforward: policy, fiduciary requirements, and high-level strategy are treated as "mandatory," but only around a quite small list of policy areas.

### Thought Leadership

Thought leadership work is focused on building capabilities. The key here is to be very selective about subject matter focus, and then to staff with high-powered players who will bring the best ideas to the business. This is the work of the "few and the fabulous," argues Cynthia McCague, Coke's former HR officer. These are not service delivery people; they are too few in number to get involved deeply in hands-on initiatives. They build capabilities the business units need in order to execute their strategies. At the corporate level, these must be capabilities that fit most or all of the businesses in the portfolio. Nancy Tennant Snyder, vice president of leadership and strategic competency development at Whirlpool, has focused her efforts on making Whirlpool the most innovative appliance company in the world, and after nearly ten years of sustained effort, Whirlpool is just that, with tangible new product results across all categories. Snyder's team's focus was on building skills, practices, and a culture deep inside the divisions (Snyder and Duarte, 2008).

Thought leaders deliver programs, best practices, new processes, consulting, and training for others to implement locally. They provide critical know-how and insights to the policymakers. Snyder argues that these teams should start small and build on quick wins with sustained focus over time. Interestingly, Snyder reports directly to the CEO, not within human resources.

The scope of these teams depends on the nature of the company's overall structure. In companies with closely related operating divisions, like Whirlpool or P&G, there are obvious points of shared capability across the units. Thought leadership functions are more difficult roles to establish in holding companies, where the interests are more diffused and the operating governance is more of a confederacy. This is part of what distinguishes GE from typical holding companies. Its ambition is to manage key talent and capital from the center—to integrate by driving managerial competence, a common culture, and best practice across its businesses.

Often, these smart people hired into the center begin to see their role as making policy, ruling on decisions, reviewing the work of the local staff, and rolling out new procedures and programs. The conflict is exacerbated when individual staff members are asked to play both a policy oversight role and a thought leadership role, and can't or don't articulate which hat they are wearing when interacting with their colleagues in the field. Where possible, oversight and thought leadership roles should be separated. The business units should also be empowered to challenge the thought leaders when they begin to stray into oversight roles, and dictate rather than enable.

The governance rule here is "optional." Business units may refuse these deliverables, but the key is to make the ideas so compelling that internal customers will be pulled to them because they are the best solutions available to solve the company's business problems.

### Selected Services

The business case for shared services is usually based on efficiency and cost. Work is brought together, standardized, and managed through a single point of accountability. Shared services can also serve an integrative function. Innovation requires ideas, freedom, and creativity. Paradoxically, it also thrives when there is a common base of organizational infrastructure that enables people from different disciplines and parts of an organization to work together seamlessly. Common communication systems, pay and reward practices, and reporting conventions all facilitate the flow of information, resources, and ideas across organizational boundaries. Shared services that create common infrastructure can facilitate this integration.

The key in shared services is to be "selective." Shared services organizations have made their way across the continents promising consolidation, automation, low-cost labor, and outsourced solutions. Sometimes they work out as planned. Often they don't.

The rule here is "mandatory participation once the businesses have signed on" to the business case. This makes it critical to get the service contract right. There are real efficiency gains to be realized from service teams located in logical geographic clusters that can service multiple business units, supported by technology. These organizations need solid business cases, reviewed in detail and endorsed by the business leaders, with payoffs that can be measured. Service contracts must be laid out in detail, committing the service delivery units to specific targets, such as cycle time, throughput, customer satisfaction, and cost per transaction.


## CENTER-LED VERSUS CENTRALIZED

Once there is a clear, contracted understanding around the value delivery framework, the options for organization structure are numerous. The HR chief in a well-known multinational company challenged design teams to avoid locating thought leadership work in the headquarters. Instead, teams completed an exhaustive inventory of internal best practices around the world. They discovered that Europe ran the best general management education programs, Latin America had seated the best practice for performance management, and the United States had implemented the most effective talent review process.

Regional practices had to be scaled up to serve as the "center" for this work. We find that distributing work in this way increases ownership on the part of the business leaders. No longer is headquarters synonymous with the center of all good ideas. Resources can remain colocated in the geographic units, which further reduces tension between the corporate function and the businesses served, and generates a much larger pool of talent from which to recruit.

The example underscores an important idea that reframes the centralized versus decentralized paradigm. *To centralize an activity is to bring control over it; to make an activity "center-led" is to bring integration to it.* The center may be a function in the headquarters, or it may be an effort by separate work centers to tie their work to a single strategy or a set of standards. For most companies today, the challenges are too complex for leaders to adhere to simple notions of centralized versus decentralized organization.

# Milestone Three Summary: Integration

*Chapter Eight: Design for Operating Governance and Chapter Nine: Allocate Power in the Matrix (Case Study)*

- Once strategic grouping is completed, design work shifts to finding ways to integrate separate units back together to create a whole. This is especially important in the matrix structure.

- The operating model of the corporation determines how closely linked the separate operating units need to be.

  - Single-business companies and those with closely inter-related products and markets usually strive to operate in a highly integrated manner.

  - Holding companies and other companies with very diversified portfolios tend to operate with little need for integration among units.

- Managing power relationships in the organization is a key design task.

- Operating governance is the process by which power is allocated across units and up and down through the levels of organization. Defining decision rights among key roles is an important part of the design process. This is a far more effective task when there is a clear operating governance framework.

- The governance levers framework (adapted from the work of Robert Simons) provides a way to define governance tactics in complex organizations. There are four key levers that should be managed to make the matrix effective:

1. Beliefs
2. Networks
3. Boundaries
4. Diagnostic measures

- Organization designers can learn to apply the tactics within each lever to ensure that the matrix organization is "tuned" to deliver the results required.

*Chapter Ten: Redesign Functions to Be Integrators*
- Corporate functions can be key integrators in large corporations, but many create confusion and frustration for the operating units. Support functions are being challenged to add more value to the business with less total cost.

- An end-to-end approach is necessary to take a holistic view of the support function on a worldwide basis, in order to ensure

  - A common strategic agenda for how value will be added
  - A consistent approach to core processes
  - Improvement of talent and skill development
  - Less allocated overhead

- The value delivery framework argues that all functional support work should be clearly designed around one of three value-adding roles. Each of the three should be distinguished from the others, and all work and staffing should be aligned to provide greater center-based leadership, without centralizing the work. The roles are

1. Function oversight and strategy
2. Thought leadership
3. Selected shared services

# MILESTONE
# FOUR

## Talent and Leadership

**MILESTONE: YOU HAVE DESIGNED AND STAFFED THE CRITICAL ROLES AND DEFINED THE WORK OF THE EXECUTIVE TEAM**

Organization design and leadership are two closely interwoven assets. When great organization and talent meet, magic is possible. One of our teachers, Walt Mahler (who was a cocreator of the GE succession planning process), argued many years ago that every time a substantial change in organization structure takes place, the top executive should rethink the talent in key management positions. Now research underscores the point. A study by the Corporate Leadership Council (CLC, 2010) argues for the importance of connecting market situations, strategy, organization design, and leadership. Among the performance gaps the CLC identified is "the legacy leader," someone well suited to the past market and organization situations, but not likely to adjust to significant changes in the market situation or the organization model going forward.

Many, if not most, general managers and CEOs we have worked with on organization design start by penciling familiar names into boxes with new titles. And often their direct reports do the same. Here's why a more thoughtful approach to leadership and organization makes sense:

- Structure changes are windows of opportunity to reconsider talent—opportunities that should not be missed. Executive teams need to be periodically refreshed and improved. Competitive environments change, strategies change, and leadership profiles should change. New, and often outside, perspectives are important.

- When organizations are redesigned, there are almost always new requirements for leader roles and behaviors, often aimed at altering old cultural norms. Those requirements need to be spelled out, and leaders need to be coached and taught to adjust.

- Not only skills and know-how but also motivational fit between incumbents and positions is critical in driving change (Charan, Drotter, and Noel, 2001). Motivational fit is a measurable and critical factor to consider in staffing a new organization.

- The most powerful form of leadership development is experience. Organization changes can be made in order to create opportunities for learning and development. And qualified candidates with the most potential should be considered for positions that are likely to produce the most learning.

Consider the example of a large security systems company that faced technology-driven changes in its markets. Security Systems, Inc. (SSI) had muddled through software development for a decade, attempting to marry IT with its traditional hardware components. It had acquired small technology companies with robust proprietary systems, and had gained very high market share in many of its markets. Creative field sales and service units around the world bundled proprietary and third-party components, on the fly, to meet the needs of their corporate customers. But the market had grown much more sophisticated, and it was critical to get beyond ad hoc bundling.

The SSI leader saw that it was now necessary to build a global capability to develop, deliver, and service complex systems solutions. A substantial reorganization emerged over several months, aimed at globalizing and strengthening the technology organization, product management, and marketing, while moving the sales organization to solutions selling.

This business model shift required the executive team to change where they spent their time and attention. Engineering leaders at SSI now had to work much more closely with marketers and had to interact directly with customers. The role of the executive team required new thinking. It needed to transition from operating as a group of individual business leaders, coming together occasionally to track results, to a team that had to cooperate closely to manage the development pipeline priorities and build bridges across geographic units, product groups, and functions in the matrix.

When significant organization changes such as these are planned, the design for talent and leadership should be part of the mix. In this part of the book, we examine how to

- Define the top-level reporting structure, design the roles of leaders, and design the work of the executive team
- Staff the talent pivot points and design the organization to develop leaders

# Design the Leadership Organization

**W**E LEARNED FROM A WISE CLIENT YEARS AGO that it is best for the top executive to be candid with incumbents at the start of a design process that he or she intends to keep options open with regard to what positions will report directly to the top, and who will fill those positions. That same executive would make calming assurances that solid performers would find a home in the new organization, but would make clear that there were no guarantees about what or where that home might be. This turned out to be a model we've seen work many times. It can be especially helpful if the leader makes clear that each person should participate in the design process with the expectation that he could end up in any role that is designed into the new structure—rather than assuming that he is designing his own future position in the business.

## DEFINE THE TOP-LEVEL
## REPORTING STRUCTURE

When the top leader is ready to make choices about what roles will sit on her direct report team, she should consider these criteria:

- Where does the executive want and need to spend time, internally and externally? (What needs the most management attention?)
- What is the extent and nature of dual reporting relationships that some team members may have with executives outside this team?
- Where do jobs need to be positioned vertically in order to have necessary influence in the organization?
- Is the executive more comfortable with a wide versus narrow span of control?
- What messages will be sent by placing given roles at the top rather than lower in the structure?

General managers of businesses, as well as functions, should be clear about how they will add the most personal value to the business. This is a judgment call that amounts to a marriage of personal skills, knowledge, and motivation with the needs of the business. One should go back to the design criteria for the organization and ask, "Where does this leader need to spend his or her time to bring these capabilities to life?"

### Options for Direct Report Structures

Let's look at three sets of alternatives that are common models for direct report structures to the CEO and general managers of large business units.

FIGURE 11.1. *The Internal Operator Option for Management Structure*

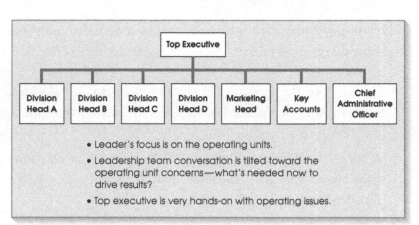

- Internal operator—when the business unit is growing, going through change, or in turnaround mode and the leader is expected to closely manage operations. See Figure 11.1.

  - All key business units, functions, and geographic units report directly to the top executive.

  - Span of control may be quite wide, or somewhat narrowed with span breakers (for example, chief of staff or chief administrative officer) for staff functions (or they may report to functional centers).

  - Management attention tends to be on activities that are most critical to growth or other mandates—from innovation to operations excellence.

  - Team members act with a high degree of independence.

- Balanced internal-external executive—when the leader wants to start building more capability among the direct report team or position one or more direct reports for succession. See Figure 11.2.

FIGURE 11.2. *The Balanced Internal-External Option for Management Structure*

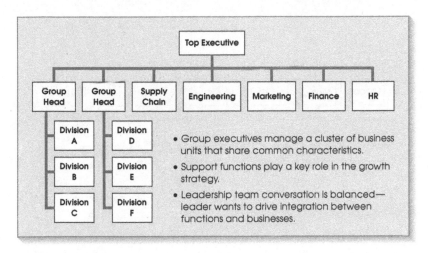

- Businesses and functions are clustered under group executives in order to allow the leader to spend time on enterprise initiatives and external interaction with customers and analysts.
- The leader may be a heavy user of one or more staff functions that are viewed as key partners in the business plan.
- Time is spent driving integration among the activities of direct reports.
- *Chief operating officer*—when the leader has a successor in place who needs to gain experience, or corporate and external responsibilities mean that most of his time and attention needs to be focused upward and outside of the unit. See Figure 11.3.
  - The top executive delegates most operating activities to a COO.
  - Typically strategy, R&D, support staff, and external stakeholder activities are managed directly by the top leader.

FIGURE 11.3. *The COO Option for Management Structure*

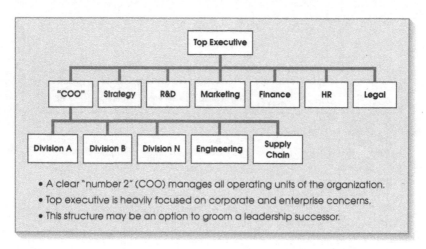

- A clear "number 2" (COO) manages all operating units of the organization.
- Top executive is heavily focused on corporate and enterprise concerns.
- This structure may be an option to groom a leadership successor.

### The Matrixed Executive Team

When a general manager finds herself managing a team with members matrixed into other areas, she needs to think differently about the composition of that team. She should try to be inclusive—to fully engage the "virtual" team members into her team—to make them feel part of her organization. The objective is for them to identify with that business.

In these circumstances, the general manager can have a quite large team—a wide span of control. In this model, the leader may not be acting as a supervisor at all for the matrixed team members. Her impact will be primarily in setting a shared vision and agenda for her business, creating high degrees of buy-in and alignment around it, and building energy and focus across the diverse membership and boundaries to get things done.

Consider again the example of Security Systems Inc. SSI's parent company placed a very bright and strategic marketing executive into the general management position of the newly formed vertical business unit. The new structure gave him direct authority for marketing, product management, and product development—the back end of the business. He was granted matrixed responsibility for the front end of the business—sales and service—which was shared with regional executives.

The SSI general manager learned over time that he could add much more value by letting the regions play the administrative and supervisory role with sales and service. He was given a powerful vote in selecting sales and service members for his team, but did not need to supervise them. In addition, he correctly reasoned that his HR and finance staff would receive functional direction from their respective disciplines. By shifting his mind-set about the core of his leadership role, he was able to elevate more product management and marketing talent to his direct report level, along with the sales and service leaders from the regions. He avoided span-breaker roles and layering, and embraced an extended team of sixteen individuals. This allowed him to have direct influence into all the key levers of his business. He could spend most of his time addressing the gaps in the product and solutions offering, while still engaging directly with the sales and service leaders to ensure that they would pull the new solutions into the markets.

## DESIGN THE ROLES OF LEADERS

Large organizations find ways to resist change. Changing behavior begins with changing the roles of the leaders. The capabilities required by the new organization should serve as the anchor point for the work of leaders. For example, a company determined to be a great brand leader needs executives who make brand a priority and bring consumer-focused ideas to the decision-making process. Incumbents must think differently about their roles or be replaced by those who will.

Such tools as success profiles and job descriptions are far more effective when they reflect the strategic needs of the business and the context of the organization design. We use three frameworks to guide our thinking when designing key roles. The *leadership pipeline* model grounds the job in the type of management and leadership work required by the role (Mahler and Drotter, 1986; Charan, Drotter, and Noel, 2001). Jaques' *requisite levels* model is useful as a way to avoid creating unnecessary layers of management in the organization (Jaques, 1989).* Finally, *span of control* provides another lens for ensuring that decision making is placed at the right level.

### Leadership Pipeline

Managerial roles are different at each level of the organization, as shown in Figure 11.4. The framework creates an integrated view of organization levels, leadership roles, and leadership talent, through a development lens. It provides a way to differentiate the intellectual and emotional demands specific to each level of leadership in the organizational pipeline. Each successive tier of leadership responsibility represents a step-function change in three elements of leadership work design and, consequently, staffing requirements:

---

*The work of Walt Mahler and Elliot Jaques has striking similarities. They were both interested in the connection between organization design and leadership. But they never met, and although they pursued parallel tracks, they apparently were not influenced by each other's work.

FIGURE 11.4. *The Leadership Pipeline Model (Also Known as Crossroads)*

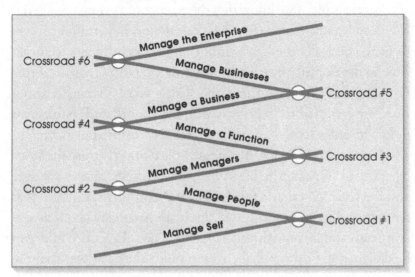

Crossroad #6

Manage the Enterprise

Manage Businesses

Manage a Business

Crossroad #5

Crossroad #4

Manage a Function

Manage Managers

Crossroad #3

Crossroad #2

Manage People

Manage Self

Crossroad #1

*Source:* Adapted from Charan, Drotter, and Noel, 2001

- Intellectual complexity
- Motivation profile (work values)
- Competency

These three job dimensions define an integrated set of roles, criteria for assessing candidates against those roles, and development road maps for future leaders.

Each time a person is promoted through an organizational "crossroad," he must make a substantial transition. He must not only demonstrate faster processing abilities and higher-order leadership skills but also set aside many of the familiar tools and practices of the old job and learn new ones. And he must change his point of view about the work. This is most evident in the transition from managing a function to managing a business, where one must focus less on familiar functional activities and invest more time and energy on working across functions and attending to customers and business results.

For example, if we know that the essence of a given managerial role is to "manage managers," we can design-in certain expectations. Generically these positions obligate incumbents to invest time in developing the leaders under them, rather than attempting to directly manage the work. Those who "manage a function" are expected to step above doing the work and to focus on policy in order to serve as thought leaders for the business.

The requirements for the role are pulled directly from the strategy of the business. The life cycle of the business shapes the role and the selection criteria for the leaders. Consider businesses that are expected to grow versus those that are essentially about generating cash and income through existing assets. Executive roles can be designed to fit those challenges in much the same way that the organization structure was designed. In businesses with a robust growth agenda, executives may be expected to be very hands-on in shaping new business models or platforms for growth. In businesses that are expected to maximize cash flow or cost reduction, executive roles will naturally emphasize operational decision making and process fixes. The selection criteria used in the executive staffing process can be aligned to ensure a good fit to the role.

### Organization Levels and Layers

The number of organization layers from the top to the bottom of the company influence what decisions are made, how quickly, and how difficult it is to navigate the organization. Many companies suffer from excess layers that accrue over time as supervisory and management positions are created to meet career path needs. The layers create inefficiencies and unnecessary approval points. Every few years a leader will be inspired to "flatten" the organization to clean out these accumulated management layers.

The late Elliott Jaques (1989) created a framework for designing the layers of an organization. He detailed an elaborate and integrated point of view on organization and leadership that established task complexity as the key criterion for determining how many layers of organization are required to manage the work of the business, and what kind of intellectual capabilities the leaders needed in order to manage the work at each level. "Ability to manage complexity" is Jaques' proxy for business intelligence, which he correctly argued was not easily measured through IQ tests. Complexity of the work is a function of the breadth of choices or optional paths to a given goal that must be considered by the incumbent or the team.

Jaques' assertion about organizational layering is provocative. He argued that there is a right (requisite) number of levels that exist in the organization. When you break business complexity down into component parts, there are a prescribed number of organization levels necessary to manage that complexity. In large multinational corporations, Jaques found six clearly distinguishable levels of work, from entry-level professionals to the CEO. The nature of work complexity at each level can be defined by its "time span"—the length of time necessary for incumbents to complete the core work and to see its effects. He argued that the work of a CEO may take ten to twenty years to fully realize. In contrast, the work of entry-level professionals can be delivered in ninety days. Figure 11.5 shows the six levels of work.

The key point is that discernable, real differences in work complexity, rather than efforts to provide pay and status or career advancement opportunities, should determine the right number of levels in the organization. Executives should create a significant time-span difference between each managerial level to eliminate the risks of overlap (ninety days, one year, two years, five years, and so forth).

FIGURE 11.5. *Requisite Levels of Work in the Multinational Corporation*

| Level | Complexity | Authority Time Span | |
|-------|------------|---------------------|---|
| VI | Long-term success depends on creating an environment for entire organization to succeed | 10–20 years | Strategic, Corporate |
| V | Judgment with constantly shifting events—intuitve and diagnostic | 5–10 years | |
| IV | Must parallel-process several interacting variables, and apply judgment to make trade-offs | 2–5 years | Integrative |
| III | Understands entire process and has preplanned ways to respond | 1–2 years | |
| II | Can reflect on potential problems and diagnose | 3–12 months | Operational |
| I | Prescribed, linear path | 90 days | |

*Source:* Adapted from Jaques, 1989

Conflicts arise in hierarchies typically because a manager and her direct reports are essentially managing the same work. The following are typical symptoms of unnecessary layers:

- There is confusion about who makes decisions.
- Higher-level managers tend to make decisions that those below them should be making.
- Communication up and down is difficult: there are too many filters, and it takes too much effort to be heard.
- Horizontal communication is difficult because there are too many "partners" to keep easily informed.
- People lack real development challenges.

As roles are defined, it is useful to apply this lens to test the real number of levels required in the organization.

### Span of Control

Span of control is the inverse partner to organization layers. As the number of layers goes up, the average number of direct reports to managers goes down, and vice versa. Excess layers of hierarchy tend to result in narrower jobs with less freedom to act. As layers are removed, job responsibilities can be widened with greater span of authority. In general, layers should be kept to a minimum.

Spans will vary, based on the breadth of cross-functional work under the leader. General managers should have narrower spans than functional managers, as the work to manage is more varied for the general managers. Having said that, we believe general managers can manage eight to ten managers quite well, and functional managers can handle more, depending on the work, the maturity of the players, and the extent of geographic diffusion.

### Span-Breaking Roles

There is often confusion about the nature of span-breaking jobs. A span-breaker position is a layer of management that exists only to reduce the span of control of the executive one level up. For example, if a general manager must manage four or five regional heads of sales and service in addition to marketing, product development, supply chain, and other functions, she may choose to have a span-breaker executive under her to whom all the regions report. The span-breaker position is not likely to create local market strategy, as each regional head must have his own. The role is not likely to manage customers or be accountable for any results other than a consolidation of the results of the team members. It is fair to say that in general these roles do not add value beyond managerial convenience for the leader.

Span breakers can add value in the form of capability building and by coaching and training the leaders below them, and they can be highly valued members of the executive team. If these outcomes are expected, the role should be designed so as not to create overlap with the managers below the span breaker.

Group executives are a case in point. In most situations, the group executive is a span breaker who oversees loosely coupled divisions. The group president is there to ensure that the right general managers are in place, that they are creating robust strategies, and that they are executing effectively on those strategies. Rarely are group strategies created unless the business units have shared customers, competitors, channels, and cost structure. But time and again we have watched as group executives argue that they must have their own finance manager, HR manager, and sometimes even an operations manager. This is a mistake. When these support positions are added, the span breaker now becomes an entire layer of infrastructure. The result, inevitably, is more cost, more bureaucratic work, and slower decisions. When the group executive is charged to actually make portfolio decisions within the assigned sector, then some form of staff support may be important. In nearly every case we know, however, that support is best provided from the center on an as-needed basis.

### Measures for Leadership Roles

Business managers who run operating units within large multinational companies are prone to focus narrowly on the results of their own divisions. Measures, pay programs, and culture reinforce these instincts. But the role of general managers or presidents of divisions in larger companies should include time and energy spent in the governance of the enterprise and in providing stewardship for key company resources. Once again, the chosen operating model should inform the extent of enterprise work that operating leaders perform, as shown in Table 11.1. In

TABLE 11.1. *The Operating Model Informs the Roles of Senior Leaders*

| I. Integrated (Single Business) | II. Divisional (Closely Related Portfolio) | III. Hybrid (Loosely Related Portfolio) | IV. Holding Company (Conglomerate) |
| --- | --- | --- | --- |
| • Linked strategy across all P&L units, with minor variations<br>• Direction from organizational "center"<br>• Common process and practices<br>• Single talent pool for leadership jobs<br>• Expectation of numerous synergies<br>• Strong centralized functions<br>• Strong corporate staff<br>• Close-knit executive committee working as an operating team<br>• Examples: Cisco, Coca-Cola, Bristol-Myers Squibb | • Complementary business portfolio and core strategies<br>• Synergies through common processes, including pooled front-end and back-end operations<br>• Resource allocation decisions made by executive committee<br>• Single-company approach to talent management<br>• Strong corporate functions supporting the business units with common policies where possible<br>• Single culture, common values, drive for synergy<br>• Examples: J&J, PepsiCo, P&G | • Common approach to setting unit strategies<br>• Few, but critical, processes and systems are common (for example, procurement, e-commerce)<br>• Some planned movement of talent across units<br>• Synergies expected only through specific shared services<br>• Value added through corporate oversight of capital, talent, and knowledge<br>• Best practices driven by corporate functions<br>• Examples: GE, Unilever, Nestlé | • Financial portfolio approach to corporate strategy and investment<br>• Financials returned to parent by business units<br>• No common processes<br>• No movement of talent across units<br>• No synergies expected<br>• Multiple cultures<br>• Small corporate staff focused on fiduciary role<br>• Examples: Berkshire Hathaway, Tyco |

general, the further to the left the company's operating model sits in the framework, the more that division leaders should be expected to be part of enterprise management.

The work of an executive team includes setting corporate strategy, teaching and mentoring key enterprise talent, overseeing corporate project teams, or coordinating cross-divisional business development initiatives. In companies such as J&J, 3M, and IBM, these are natural extensions of the general manager's role. In many other companies, these tasks are considered distractions from "running my business." If the enterprise work is expected of the division head, these expectations need to be spelled out and measured, or the result is quite frustrating for many, often including the CEO.

Getting the measures right is important in defining leadership roles. In our experience, a functional manager typically should be accountable primarily for elements that he or she can directly influence. For example, a procurement manager is accountable for the cost of purchased materials. A general manager, in contrast, should be held accountable for a broad mix of results reflecting a range of trade-off decisions he might make. General managers are often given too broad or too narrow a span of accountability. In the matrix, this issue is critical because the head of a global business unit (product, category, or customer) does not control all of the elements in the trade-off decisions she might make to drive profitable growth, but should have very substantial influence if she has the right leadership skills. She should be measured as if she had those skills.

Compensation program designs tend to lag during the organization redesign process. When roles are redesigned, the measures and the pay programs need to reflect these changes.

# DESIGN THE WORK OF THE EXECUTIVE TEAM

Executive teams in many companies struggle with how closely knit as a team they need to be. Many executives are aggravated by long and frequent meetings that seem to produce little tangible benefit; others are frustrated that there are no meetings at all. In many cases, executives who run support functions are disappointed with the lack of teamwork, whereas operating executives see little value in forcing it when they are held accountable mainly for the results of their own unit.

Many executive "teamwork" problems are directly related to the fact that there may be no clear reason for the executive committee to be a team. The more business unit or market diversity that exists in the organization and the more its executives manage relatively autonomous units, the more they struggle with how they should spend their time together.

Whether the direct reports to the leader need to be a true team, or merely function as a group, depends on the extent of interdependence of their work and, therefore, the extent of integration required among their separate tasks (Nadler and Spencer, 1998). Here again, the operating model of the business informs the nature of the work of the executive committee.

Time spent building a team with a collection of executives who manage very separate and autonomous divisions is often time wasted. But in most companies it is not a binary choice to become a team or a group. Leadership teams that choose to spend very little time together, due to *apparent* lack of interdependence, (1) often fail to manage the links among "autonomous" units, (2) often suffer weak corporate functions, (3) tend to watch as conflicts in the matrix rage, and (4) lack a cohesive approach to shaping a single culture in the overall company.

Designing the executive team role, membership, and structure is an important part of organization design. A continuum of value-adding roles should be considered. The options for the work of the executive team range from strongly operations-oriented tasks and decision making on one end, to visionary and relationship-building tasks on the other, as shown in Figure 11.6. The top executive will have personal preferences, but the approach to strategic grouping and the operating governance model of the

FIGURE 11.6. *A Continuum of Potential Roles for the Executive Team*

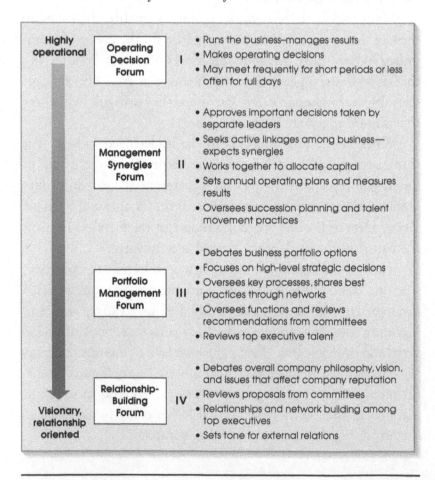

| Highly operational | Operating Decision Forum | I | • Runs the business–manages results<br>• Makes operating decisions<br>• May meet frequently for short periods or less often for full days |
| | Management Synergies Forum | II | • Approves important decisions taken by separate leaders<br>• Seeks active linkages among business—expects synergies<br>• Works together to allocate capital<br>• Sets annual operating plans and measures results<br>• Oversees succession planning and talent movement practices |
| | Portfolio Management Forum | III | • Debates business portfolio options<br>• Focuses on high-level strategic decisions<br>• Oversees key processes, shares best practices through networks<br>• Oversees functions and reviews recommendations from committees<br>• Reviews top executive talent |
| Visionary, relationship oriented | Relationship-Building Forum | IV | • Debates overall company philosophy, vision, and issues that affect company reputation<br>• Reviews proposals from committees<br>• Relationships and network building among top executives<br>• Sets tone for external relations |

business should inform the work of the top team, both at the corporate level and often in the major divisions as well.

Recall the four governance levers for balancing power in the matrix organization that we discussed in Milestone Three: Integration.

1. Beliefs
2. Networks
3. Boundaries
4. Diagnostic measures

It is the core work of the executive team to manage the governance levers in the matrix organization. It is hard work, and many executive teams do not have the patience for it; but the investment of energy here delivers high return on management time. We can think of executive teams along a spectrum, as shown in Table 11.2. In the following sections, we define each type of executive team and discuss which governance levers are most important to each.

*Operating Decisions Forum.*    This is often the choice of highly integrated, single-business companies where the executive team

TABLE 11.2. *The Four Types of Executive Teams and the Extent to Which They Utilize the Four Governance Levers at the Corporate Level*

|  | Type of Executive Committee | | | |
| --- | --- | --- | --- | --- |
|  | *I. Operating Decisions Forum* | *II. Management Synergies Forum* | *III. Portfolio Management Forum* | *IV. Relationship-Building Forum* |
| **Four Levers** | | | | |
| Beliefs | High | High | Moderate | Moderate |
| Networks | Moderate | High | Moderate | Moderate |
| Boundaries | Moderate | High | Moderate | Low |
| Diagnostic measures | High | High | Moderate | Low |

serves as the operating leadership of the company. But some very large multiproduct companies operate in this fashion as well. Apple and Mars are good examples. Strategic linkages among units are strong, and the need for integrated decisions is high. This is a true management team, where interactions among operating and functional leaders need to be close and effective.

For this type of team, the most effective governance levers are likely to be simple belief systems and diagnostic measures. Networks and boundaries are less important due to the hands-on nature of this operating team. Governance and the work are one and the same.

*Management Synergies Forum.*   This type of team is suited to multidivision companies that want synergy among separate operating units, or that utilize shared back-end (product or operations) or front-end (sales and service) functions. Divisions are treated as somewhat autonomous strategic business units, but active linkages and power balancing among them are emphasized. The executive team works to set annual operating plans, allocate capital, and monitor key measures for the shared results. The team is actively engaged in managing talent development and moves across the operating units. The need for trust, effective communications, and power sharing is high.

These executive teams need to utilize all four of the governance levers actively. They are likely to share common beliefs through extensive face-to-face interaction. Meetings are likely to be shorter and more frequent. They utilize networks and councils for global business initiatives, executive talent programs, and process improvement. Boundary management is critical: teams should be quite active in clarifying decision rights across businesses and functions, aligning P&Ls and budgets, and overseeing critical policy areas. Diagnostic measures are managed through an integrated business dashboard that includes a balanced view of financials along with customer measures, people measures, and process effectiveness.

*Portfolio Management Forum.*   This team operates in multi-division companies that require few synergies among the businesses. This executive group meets on a regular basis, but usually not more than once every other month for one or more full days. Agendas are more project or initiative focused. This group acts like an operating board to review subcommittee proposals in the management of the overall portfolio, including acquisitions. They may identify some opportunities for synergy among the business units, but the units are usually fairly autonomous. Functions such as finance, HR, and IT are usually active in driving a few key integrating initiatives, such as functional talent management.

This kind of executive group can be quite challenging. This is a marginal team; there are reasons for members to interact effectively, but the points of interdependence are few. The matrix may be primarily between businesses and support functions. A shared set of beliefs is important, including a common view about the operating model and the role of functions. These teams find networks to be useful in a few key initiatives. Diagnostic measures tend to be concentrated on the overall financial performance of the portfolio and a few integrative initiatives and functions, such as shared services for support activities.

*Relationship-Building Forum.*   This is an executive group that leads business units with little commonality in business model, customers, or operations. The need for teamwork is low. Primary interactions are between functional leaders and each operating unit head, based on explicit or implied service contracts.

Even so, common beliefs and a few interactive networks can be quite useful, especially with regard to how the corporation will manage its relations with external stakeholders. Boundaries and diagnostic measures, however, are managed primarily inside the separate operating units.

# CHAPTER 12

# Make the Right Talent Choices

ORGANIZATION REDESIGN IS A WINDOW OF OPPORTUNITY TO bring more or different talent into the business. Building substantially new capabilities often entails changes in talent. One of the biggest regrets we hear voiced by leaders after completing an organization design change is that they didn't act courageously or swiftly enough on the difficult talent decisions. They were too quick to fill critical positions with subpar players rather than look externally or hold the job open until the right person could be found. We encourage a mind-set that ensures that the right people are in the right seats when the redesign is complete.

## STAFF THE TALENT PIVOT POINTS

The capabilities and the design criteria, established in the Business Case and Discovery phase, should inform the staffing needs. Talent needs should be judged against the forces that are bringing change to the business. But not all positions in the new organization need the same degree of attention. We are believers in the power of asymmetrical investment in talent. Investments in new skills should not be allocated equally because not all jobs have an equal impact on the capabilities you seek. The concept of *pivot points* argues for focus on those few, targeted skill sets in the new organization that will have a disproportionate impact on results (Boudreau and Ramstad, 2007).

We recently worked with a CEO and his top team to launch a new set of succession planning and development practices. The HR officer did a terrific job of articulating the case for a robust talent agenda to support the growth plans of the business. The CEO felt strongly about the subject, and he insisted that all his top executives be certain they had only "A players" on their teams. The intention was right, but in the first talent review meeting, it became clear that at best this was a goal that would take years to achieve. Further, such an effort would actually be quite impractical and would divert time and resources from other investments. The lesson is that not all positions require A players.

Rather than attempting to develop all leaders equally, asymmetrical investing argues for a targeted approach. Each company has a unique set of talent "hot spots" that if staffed properly, create competitive advantage in their context. Figure 12.1 shows some examples. Apple, as another example, has made it an obsession to constantly scout externally for creative designers and software developers, whether or not there are active job openings.

There are five key questions that need to be answered in building a staffing plan for critical talent:

- What are the talent pivot points in this new organization?
- Where will we make changes in staffing?
- What are the decision ground rules? Where will we not compromise? How wide will we cast the net for candidates?

FIGURE 12.1. *Examples of Talent "Pivot Points" in Various Companies*

| | Sources of Competitive Advantage | Talent Needs | Organization Needs |
|---|---|---|---|
| Nestlé | Brand presence in emerging markets | Marketers with experience in emerging markets—more local national players | Top markets elevated to CEO—dedicated infrastructure |
| CISCO | New product ideas for new applications | Marketing-savvy engineers who can work in teams | Cross-business teams turned loose with seed money—empowerment |
| STARBUCKS COFFEE | "The Starbucks Experience" | Baristas and store managers | Achieve best employee experience—translate to consumer experience |
| GE | State-of-the-art management systems across diverse portfolio | Global pool of best mobile general management talent | The right set of P&L units for portfolio visibility—fast acquisition integration |

*Source:* Adapted from Boudreau and Ramstad, 2007

- What is the process we will employ to generate candidates, assess them, and select them into jobs?
- How will we communicate continuously with the stakeholders?

Companies often have past practices they look to for staffing during a reorganization. These are often associated with bad memories of downsizing exercises and, if so, should be avoided.

We advocate strongly for a process that includes some form of rigorous assessment of candidates for all jobs that have substantially changed (greater than 50 percent of job content is a good rule). Job slotting is an option for people whose roles change little. The degree of disruption must be balanced with the opportunity to raise the level of performance. The details of the staffing process cannot be resolved until it is clear (1) what positions have changed, (2) what positions have been created, (3) what positions have been eliminated, and (4) which people are affected by these changes. We also strongly urge the most transparent approach to staffing that is possible. Openness about the candidate pools, the selection criteria, and the assessment methods is critical to maintaining trust.

## REPURPOSE RESOURCES

Our experience over the past several years with many companies reinforces research that shows the limiting effects of spreading or cutting resources equally across the organization. Reorganizations are opportunities to *disrupt the equality* that evolves in asset allocation. Unlike across-the-board reductions in headcount, repurposing resources requires hard decisions, and few companies do it well. Repurposing becomes especially important when the new design requires investment to drive new opportunities—investment that must be funded internally.

The thought process must start with a shared understanding among the executive team of where each business unit is in its life cycle. Although legacy businesses tend to generate most of the income and profit, and therefore must have some degree of profit protection, the bias must be to starve resources out of those franchises to fund new ones, or the organization cannot grow.

The objectives of repurposing resources in a given company might include these:

- Meet the resource requirements of higher-growth activities (especially for new business models) without increasing the current people costs of the business

- Identify mission-critical work for each function and business, and rationalize current roles and staffing levels to focus on that work

- Identify budgeted resources in functions and businesses that can be shifted to growth activities to fund incremental needs

- Eliminate unnecessary complexity and redundancy in order to move faster and make quicker decisions (for example, reduce role overlap between center-based and geographic functional units)

- Strengthen talent and skill sets for all critical or pivot roles

- Accelerate the effectiveness of end-to-end function designs, including increased efficiency and effectiveness of support resources

If executive teams could start with a clean sheet of paper, few would choose to allocate resources in the manner of the status quo. But companies rarely take a clean-sheet approach to balancing resources because of the power issues involved, the potential for upsetting the organization, and the sheer hard work required to do it. Decisions about repurposing can't be handed to a consultant or delegated with the organization. This is a hands-on task for the executive team that requires decision data, courage, and good judgment.

Here are the practices we believe are most productive:

- Establish a set of objectives and a set of principles to guide the process. Be clear about what new resources are required to fund new growth opportunities. Set a target to fund them with no increases in cost. Be clear that the focus is on building new capabilities for new growth opportunities.

- Pull the quantitative data on current headcounts and costs and make the numbers as visible as possible by level in each function, department, and geographic unit.

- Consider having the HR or OD staff lay out a short qualitative situation analysis with regard to current

  - Bottlenecks and areas of slow decision making

  - Areas of role confusion and conflict

  - Gaps in capability and skill sets

- Welcome an open review of the data by the entire executive team, if possible. Use the objectives to conduct open questioning of all current resource allocations. (Teams that do not have the mutual trust needed for them to be candid can set the stage for further dialogue by laying out the data on wall charts and using yellow sticky dots to identify areas they want to question and red ones for areas they want to challenge.)

- Identify hypotheses for possible repurposing of resources along the way. Build out the options without evaluating them the first time around. Some teams find it useful to establish categories that define the impact of jobs on the growth agenda.

- When possible, tie the discussions to talent planning sessions; be maniacal about the idea of "getting better" at growth.

- Capture conclusions and build a repurposing plan into the larger transition milestone planning.

Repurposing is an obvious opportunity when end-to-end functions are redesigned. The framework presented in Chapter

Ten that articulates three value-based roles for center-led functions (policy and strategy, thought leadership, and selected shared services) can be used to categorize the current resources for the entire function around the world. Once executive teams are able to secure the headcount information, they often find that it is quite enlightening to see in what work the resources are engaged.

## Design the Organization to Grow Leaders

The right set of experiences is the most important influence on leadership development (Corporate Leadership Council, 2003; Kesler, 2002; Charan, Drotter, and Noel, 2001). The leadership pipeline model outlines broad paths of experience, from entry level to enterprise management, that can be used to select, guide, and develop high performers. This view of leadership development argues that a company can grow better senior leaders if it

1. Assesses a leader's potential against the unique needs of the next organizational crossroad (intellectual ability, skills, and motivation fit)
2. Develops leaders by providing the right experiences through multiple crossroads
3. Supports people through those transitions—with the right coaching and learning programs as they pass through a crossroad

Many companies identify general management depth as a strategic capability, directly affecting their ability to execute growth strategies. Most hope to populate top executive succession plans, including future potential candidates to replace the CEO, from within. But many companies face a general management talent gap and can't produce executive-level leadership fast enough.

Companies that demonstrate the most progress in growing general managers, such as IBM, Schlumberger, Honeywell, and General Electric, take risks on the right people early in their careers so as to provide experience with profit and loss, customer management and leading large teams (Arons and Ruh, 2004; Corporate Leadership Council, 2003). In general, they follow a common set of development principles:

- Create opportunities for people who have potential to make one or more substantial upward moves

- Delegate real responsibility and hold people accountable for sustained results

- Test highest-potential leaders frequently and take increasing risks on those who succeed by moving them across functions, markets, and business models

In response to these and other insights, IBM has retooled its practices to rate candidate readiness in terms of "positions-to-readiness" rather than the typical "years-to-readiness," stressing development actions that must be taken.

Companies that are successful at growing a deep bench of general manager candidates focus on the developmental assignments at each career crossroad. As the nature of general management jobs varies within a given company, so does the development value of these roles. The value of a given experience depends on what the business needs from its leaders—what kinds of decisions it will call on them to make as they move ahead with their growth plans (Kesler and Kirincic, 2005). Typical high-value experiences include exposure to

- Strategic complexity

- International markets and cultures, especially emerging markets

- Leading large teams
- Managing a P&L
- Varied business models
- Operational complexity
- Start-ups and turnaround situations

Most companies make some use of these situations to develop leaders. We encourage companies to consider how they can turn them into more systemic development experiences and, better yet, how they can use organization design work to increase the number of roles that contain these high-value challenges.

## CASE STUDY—TALENT AND ORGANIZATION

A well-known consumer brand company recently decided to solve a leadership talent problem and an organization problem in an integrated fashion. CPG Brands (a fictional name of a real company) had long been organized at an enterprise level around a small number of global brands on one axis of the matrix, and a very powerful regional structure on the other. Power was vested largely in thirty regional general managers, who supervised a total of 120 country managers. Above the powerful regional general managers sat five group presidents, who reported directly to the COO of the company. Although the group presidents were senior, most of the operating decision making was vested in the regional general manager positions. When the COO of the company wanted to know what was happening in his worldwide markets, he telephoned them directly.

An organization design initiative concluded that it was essential to eliminate a layer of regional management by realigning into a new set of geographic clusters. This change merged a number of regional management roles. The effect of the proposed change was to widen spans of control at all levels, while consolidating geographic infrastructure and support functions where doing so made the most sense, sometimes at the regional level and sometimes at the group level.

Separately a team of HR and general managers had completed a diagnostic study on key talent gaps in the global general management leadership pipeline of the business—a response to a number of frustrating internal searches for A players to fill critical positions. It became obvious that the two initiatives influenced each other in important ways. We worked with the executive committee to define an integrated problem statement:

---

## PROBLEM STATEMENT—CPG BRANDS

- There are too many regional P&L units (regional general manager assignments) in the business: shifts in key growth centers require fewer units with more scale and resources in-market; the cost of regional and group infrastructure is not sustainable; and role confusion between region and group creates unnecessary complexity.
- Regional general manager positions vary widely in scale and complexity, but the current three tiers of roles are defined only by current revenue and do not reflect growth potential, value to the business, or value to global leadership development.
- Today's group presidents do not have adequate breadth and depth of experience in brand marketing, portfolio strategy, and corporate governance. Rather, they are focused
  *(Continued)*

---

---

### PROBLEM STATEMENT—CPG BRANDS (CONTINUED)

narrowly on sales, distribution management, and operations management. There is no path of career experiences for developing group presidents who can be fully effective in today's markets and compete as future COO candidates.
- Lateral moves are not valued by the business or the general managers.
- Delayering the geographic organization could have the effect of further exacerbating the lack of development experiences.

---

It was clear in the problem statement how the organization and leadership talent challenges interacted. CPG's rich heritage as a multinational and its strong core brands provided exceptional opportunities to expose a cadre of mobile, international executives to learning experiences. The key was to make learning a priority in the way new roles and the relationships among them were defined.

The first task was to clarify the differences among the proposed general management roles in a way that reflected both their value to the business (as a basis for market-based job evaluation) and their value to global leadership development. Attempts were made to sort the positions on the basis of such criteria as market development, growth potential, current revenue, complexity of the regulatory environment, and diversity of external stakeholder interests. In consideration of the anticipated leadership challenges, the team developed a two-by-two grid that juxtaposed the state of geographic market development with leadership task complexity. A set of criteria defined each of the axes in the matrix:

*Decision Complexity Criteria*
- Single-country versus multicountry region
- Functional scope of direct reports
- Political and regulatory factors
- Special strategic challenges and difficulties due to past history

*State of Market Development Criteria*
- Extent of trade development (account size and international reach)
- Sophistication and diversity of distribution channels
- Current volumes and profitability
- Nature of marketing mix

Growth potential in the market was a third dimension that was overlaid across the matrix. Countries were sorted into the four quadrants with high-growth prospects highlighted. The four cells called out the most essential differences in the markets from the point of view of leadership requirements.

Next the team identified the essential experiences that a group president should have, in order to guide general managers through the right experience path. Figure 12.2 illustrates the essential experiences on the grid. The ovals indicate different types of market experiences. The conclusion of the team was that all leaders who aspired to become group presidents needed to hold positions in at least two of the three ovals as well as to hold a position in senior marketing or customer management. Later the team identified requisite field experiences for aspiring general managers as well.

Over time, the team developed a set of planning, selection, and coaching tools, to guide job moves. CPG used the framework to guide staffing and succession planning decisions

FIGURE 12.2. *CPG Co. Regional GM Positions, Sorted in Terms of the Development Experiences That Each Position Offers*

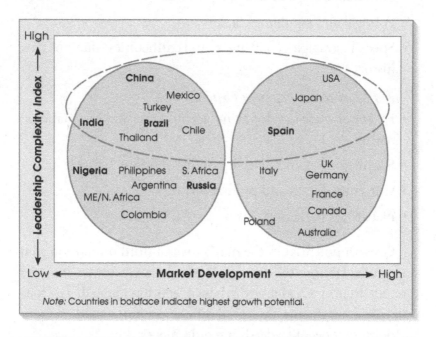

*Note:* Countries in boldface indicate highest growth potential.

that could do a better job of selecting candidates with an eye to developing future top executives. In this way, organization structure, leadership roles, and leadership development became part of one integrated design.

# Milestone Four Summary: Talent and Leadership

*Chapter Eleven: Design the Leadership Organization*
- The operating model of the company and the capabilities you seek to build should be used to design the leadership structure and roles.

- There are a number of options for designing the reporting relationships of the top management team. The best option will be based on such factors as where the top executive wants to spend his or her time, the scope of the roles of direct reports, where jobs need to be placed in order for them to be effective, and comfort with wide as opposed to narrow spans of control.

- The roles of individual leaders must be defined with an integrated view of the overall work to be done and a focus on the strategic goals of the business.

- The leadership pipeline model and other frameworks can help clearly distinguish the roles of executives and managers at each level of the business.

- Organization levels should be consciously designed to fit the complexity of the work. In most cases, no more than six levels are needed from the entry-level professional to the CEO.

- The role of the executive team should be defined in order to make it clear what the work of the team or group will be when executives are together. There are four types of executive committees. The operating model of the company largely determines whether an executive committee should be a tightly knit team, a collection of individual members, or something in between.

*Chapter Twelve: Make the Right Talent Choices*

- Staffing the new organization should be viewed as a critical window of opportunity to increase the overall talent depth in the business and to ensure that the right people are in the right positions going forward.

- Pivot positions—those that have a disproportionate impact on business results—should receive the greatest scrutiny. Talent for these critical roles should be sourced from the best internal and external pools.

- Most companies today need to think hard about shifting resources from yesterday's work to activities that will also deliver future growth. Such a shift requires tough decisions and discipline. Every effort should be made to force a review of positions and talent so as to repurpose scarce resources where they can have the most impact.

- Organization design offers a great opportunity to grow leaders. Experience paths can be built into the organization to ensure that emerging leaders are exposed to variations in business complexity, international markets, business models, and team size and maturity.

# MILESTONE
# FIVE

## Transition

### MILESTONE: YOU ARE LEADING THE CHANGE AND ARE PREPARED TO MEASURE, LEARN, AND ADJUST

The announcement is not the finish line. This observation, made by one our clients, is a reminder that the work of organization design does not end with decisions on structure, process, and staffing. The quality of the transition to the new envisioned future state is as important as the quality of the design decisions.

The Corporate Leadership Council (2010) has found that when organizational structure changes do not achieve desired results, there are often three primary reasons. First, leaders are unclear as to their roles and unsure of their goals and objectives and how those have changed in the new organization. They revert to old, familiar behaviors and patterns. Second, change disrupts decision-making processes, creating uncertainty about authority. Decisions and innovation slow. Third, employee information networks break down. Professional relationships with colleagues are severed. Management access to information decreases, and the ability to coordinate across the business suffers, even though the intention of the design may have been to increase collaboration. Structure changes change old patterns of behavior, but are not enough, on their own, to build new ones.

Our premise when working with an organization is that we are shaping the next phase of growth, not merely fixing the current state. We are not just changing; we are building something new. Too often, good designs underperform because the job of transition wasn't finished. The organization was changed, but it wasn't rebuilt.

Most executives today want to drive changes in culture, behavior, and skills as part of a planned transition to new capabilities. These deeper changes may take twenty-four to thirty-six months to effect. When design changes are more complex, it is very important to clarify a destination. Implementation or transition is a series of steps that move the organization toward the future state. At each juncture there is opportunity to learn and fine-tune.

When changing an organization, it is impossible to plan for all potential situations, flip a switch to go live, and expect all to work perfectly. Rather we suggest using an implementation planning approach that seeks to anticipate 80 percent of what needs to change, focuses on the critical points of leverage, communicates with employees honestly, and builds in feedback and adjustments along the way. This period can range from a few months to a few years, depending on the complexity of change and how fast the leader believes the change needs to occur.

This part of the book is organized into two chapters to

- Guide you in setting a destination for the change, determining the pace, and sequencing the major shifts of power change
- Assist in developing a plan for how the executive team can best manage the transition work

# Set the Implementation Plan

T O SUBSTANTIALLY REALIGN AN ORGANIZATION REQUIRES a well-sequenced and well-paced set of relatively complex tasks. Some of the tasks may be projects in and of themselves, tied together into a larger program. Galbraith's Star Model is a good place to start in identifying the list of tasks that need to be managed. Each point of the star may contain many implementation items, ranging from substantial reengineering of processes and realigning of reward systems to launching new teams, reallocating physical space, and evaluating job descriptions. The details become very important, needless to say. First, however, it is critical to envision a clear picture of the destination.

## DEFINING A DESTINATION

It's not unusual to hear middle managers during a major organizational realignment say, "There are so many moving parts right now—so many unanswered questions about how all the pieces will add up. I wish we could get a clearer picture of where we are going."

Sometimes it is difficult to be definitive about the end-state of organization design; what looks like the right flight formation today may be different in three years. But the target—a foreseeable destination—can and should be defined. Candid communication about the future state enhances the credibility of the process and helps avoid the perception that leaders are lurching from one idea to the next. Better to tell what is known, be candid about what is not, and then keep the lines of two-way communication open.

It is also okay to qualify the destination as "our best estimate at this point in time." Often what looks like the logical end state feels like a bridge too far. The journey may be so filled with obstacles and arguments against a full realignment that management decides to set an interim target, with the intent to evaluate further options later. The option for more aggressive change is left open, to be determined by how fast capabilities are developed and by the rate of change in the external market.

Figure 13.1 shows the continuum of choices available to a medical products company that sought to shift from a primarily geographic organization to a strong product and customer matrix. The continuum represents options ranging from the status quo to a radically altered operating model and organization design. This kind of graphic can be quite useful to illustrate the realignment journey. In the case of the medical products company, management demonstrated courage and clarity by sinking a stake in the ground for realignment over a two-year period; and executives were candid about pointing out that they would learn as they went and would determine whether they would continue further along the continuum once the first destination was reached.

FIGURE 13.1. *Example of a Two-Year Destination and a Longer-Term Destination for Organization Realignment at a Medical Products Company*

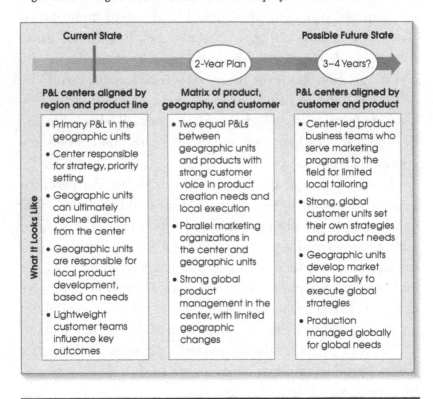

There are many arguments for laying out a destination and a story to go with it during the change process. When there are gaps in the story, people who feel anxious are prone to fill in those gaps. The worst thing is for management to withhold information about a likely future state while incrementally working their way toward it. But perhaps the more important role of a clear destination and set of progress points is the need to keep the executive team focused on its work managing the transition.

## STAGING AND PACING THE MAJOR TASKS

In nearly every reorganization initiative we've been part of over the years, there were voices in the management ranks who argued for moving in measured steps and avoiding traumatic, sudden changes; and nearly always there were those who argued persuasively that speed was critical—that pulling the Band-Aid off slowly would be more painful than a quick tug. The leader must choose a course that works for the business. The reality is, however, that the pace of change in the external environment pushes most businesses we know to move at a faster rate than the executive team is comfortable with.

### *The "Big Bang" Versus Phased Approach*

The chosen approach is influenced by the fundamental reason for change. If the company is currently healthy but the design change is driven by an anticipated change in strategy (new technologies or new competitors), then evolution can work well. Evolving over time to the new state, rather than abruptly changing everything, is less unsettling to employees, allows time to build new capabilities, and creates an orderly transition from the current core business to the new sources of growth and profitability.

However, there are two circumstances where a "pull the Band-Aid off fast" approach may be warranted. In the first case, a clear change in direction of the business has begun, and the structure works against the new strategy. If the strategy choices are clear and competitive pressures make it critical to move swiftly to recover market share or stem financial losses, it often makes sense to move fast. Basic structure changes may come first in order to create clear ownership for driving new capabilities. Then work streams can be established to work through the other change tracks and implementation details.

The second situation in which a fast realignment often makes sense is when an external change has already occurred and the current organization design actually gets in the way of making the right strategy choices for the future. This is a case where structure needs to precede strategy. This situation often occurs when strategic business units that were well suited to the past are now obstacles to holistic, market-focused thinking and decision making. A significant and visible change is needed to shake up the organization so that new energy is released, new conversations take place, and different decisions are made.

### Does a Pilot Make Sense?

Conducting a pilot consists of choosing one area to change first while the rest of the organization remains in the current state. The appeal of a pilot is that it keeps the risk of change contained. The key is to be clear as to why you would use a pilot. Are you performing an experiment, where there is a real possibility of changing course after the pilot? Or are you determined to move ahead, but seek to learn on a smaller scale before full implementation?

A pilot is useful only when there is a contained unit that is composed of all or most of the elements of the larger system. For example, if the design will change the structure across a regional customer service organization, it could be useful to pilot the change in one region, learn and adjust, and then make the change in the other regions. In contrast, if the new design covers an entire business unit, then a pilot is unlikely to be a fair test. For example, if the design changes the relationship between regional customer service centers and a centralized customer care operation, the single region can't change without the whole system changing. This kind of pilot is likely to be an exercise in frustration; a failure at the pilot site may be taken as a flaw in the design logic, and the change abandoned for the wrong reason.

If there is a compelling reason to change the organization, and running a pilot will yield only limited learning and delay important business results, then a full and coordinated implementation is probably a better approach.

### Sequencing the Transition

Pace is not the only issue, and focusing on it can be misleading. Structure change can be a blunt instrument to realign power and behaviors. As we've discussed, sometimes structure change is purposefully used to signal a major shift in strategy and to break familiar and comfortable, but no longer effective, decision patterns. If the organization change is systemic, however, it may even make sense to change structure last. Realigning processes to change work flows, changing the rules about who makes key decisions, changing metrics to encourage and reward different behaviors, or developing the skills that will underlie needed capabilities may be the place to start.

It is important to think about the sequencing or staging of the major events. The key is to sort out so-called critical path items—those changes that must come first for the others to be successful. Sometimes it is clear what the sequence should be, and sometimes it is a judgment call; there is no formula. Again, a smart place to start is to call out the major blocks of change, using Galbraith's Star Model as the lens. The executive team can work its way around the star and ask itself, "Do any of these design pieces have to be implemented first before others can be successful?"

The major blocks of transition are likely to include

- Direct report structure to the top executive
- Structure at lower levels or within subunits

- A major business process implementation or redesign
- Realignment of information and reporting systems
- Physical relocation of units or an entire business
- A major realignment of skill sets
- Realignment of metrics and reward systems

Once the major blocks of change have been sequenced and the detailed action items under each have been identified, they need to be placed on a calendar. Gantt charts are the favored tool. A sample is shown in Figure 13.2. A Gantt chart is basically a bar chart that illustrates a project schedule, posting the start and finish dates for each activity. It is helpful to begin by completing a high-level view that is used to debate the basic sequencing and timing, then to build out a much more detailed version to validate timing estimates.

### Examples of Transition Planning

In order to illustrate how the implementation approach should fit the strategic need and context, we present two examples.

*The Systems Integrator.* One of our clients designed a new global business unit to act as an integrated systems business unit inside a larger business group. The structure changes seemed relatively straightforward, but a review using the Star Model revealed a critical path item that needed to precede the shift in structure. A major shift in solutions-selling skills was required in the sales organization. Changing the skill set of the sales force would not be an easy task. Faced with a twelve- to eighteen-month delay in launching the new unit, the general manager negotiated an arrangement with the group president to hire in a small number of systems salespeople who could help launch the

FIGURE 13.2. *A Typical High-Level Gantt Chart for an Organization Realignment over a Six-Month Period*

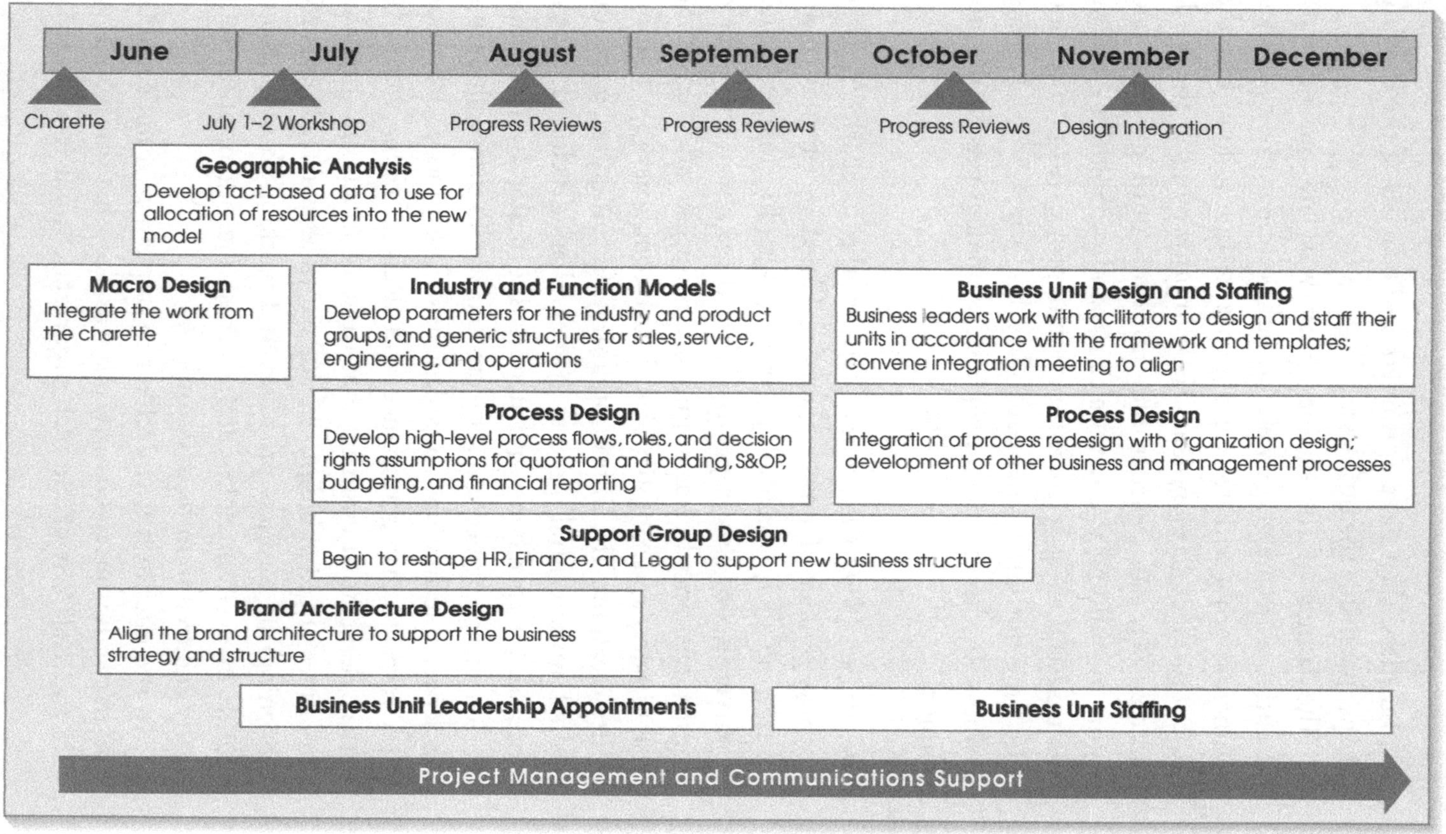

new business, then serve as trainers and coaches of the existing salespeople inside the business.

The launch of the business unit was laid out in steps. Executive team members were brought on board in a planned manner, starting with the head of marketing, followed by the head of product development. Their organizations in the headquarters were not restructured, however, until progress had begun in building the new sales capability. Solutions selling was undertaken as a cross-functional project to ensure that it became not just a sales capability but a new way of doing business. In this example, people development preceded other changes.

*The Power Plant Contractor.*   In another scenario, a large Japanese builder of power plants realigned its business units focused on global technology into geographic market units. However, it was also imperative that these newly empowered regional customer business units use common processes in the areas of safety and compliance and have common project profitability measures. The shift in organization could not be accomplished until central process owners had developed robust processes for specifying and negotiating major contracts and for delivering engineering projects that would draw value from the separate technology organizations. The process definition work revealed that governance and decision rights would be critical elements in ensuring that these contracts and projects, sometimes priced at billions of dollars, were managed properly. Designing the business processes and working through many rounds of decision rights drafts across the organization took nearly eighteen months to complete.

In the interim it was decided to implement a pilot market unit in two European countries. It was clear that this would not be a full-scale test of the new organization, but it was agreed that meaningful learning could occur that would benefit the larger rollout later, especially with regard to resourcing these regional market units and learning how local leaders needed to coordinate between their customers and the corporate technology centers. In this example, the process changes led implementation, and a pilot of structure change was used as a testing and learning opportunity.

# CHAPTER 14

# Navigate the Transition

COMPANIES THAT FINISH THE PLAY ON ORGANIZATION design are distinguished by executive teams that do the hard work of leading the transition all the way through. One chief executive made the case to his executive committee recently, "The framing is up on our new organization. But as I see it, the plumbing and electrical systems will take another year to install, and then there will be adjustments required for another year after that." He dedicated nearly one full staff meeting every month to managing the transition for the first year after people were realigned in new roles, and he kept transition topics on every agenda for a second full year to adjust power relationships in the complex matrix the team was putting in place.

The performance of the new organization was exceptional within the first eighteen months. Great reserves of energy were funneled into the major growth opportunities, and the diverse cast of characters in the matrix worked hard to manage the conflicts with creativity and to follow through. The chief executive made it clear at the beginning that there was no turning back, but he was in the trenches working the levers with his direct reports to make the new organization work as he envisioned it would.

## LEADING TRANSITION—THE WORK

As soon as a basic transition plan is struck, the executive team should participate in a launch workshop that lays out a leadership agenda for the first thirty to ninety days, with high-level placeholders for the subsequent three to nine months. This agenda will be refreshed over time, and the details obviously vary by company and situation, but there are always plenty of things to do in the first thirty to ninety days. Figure 14.1 illustrates a straw model of transition items that are common during the first twelve months of a substantial reorganization.

### First Thirty to Ninety Days: The Launch

The launch of the reconfigured executive team is a major item on the project Gantt chart, as it initiates the ongoing routines for running the organization change project as well as managing the business. After the design work is complete, new executive teams are eager to get back to running the company. However, their effectiveness as a leadership body will determine, to a large degree, how smooth and successful the transition phase will be. Before the new executive team settles into a regular meeting pattern, the first few meetings should be carefully designed and facilitated. Each member should receive his or her own "master design book" that contains all the key design documents, including design criteria, organization charts, missions, role definitions, and draft decision rights. This can be a low-tech binder of materials, with pages that are replaced frequently over the first ninety days of implementation.

FIGURE 14.1. *Typical Implementation and Transition Activities in a Major Reorganization Initiative*

| The Launch<br>First 30–90 Days | Momentum<br>Months 3–6 | Learning and Adjusting<br>Months 6–12 and Beyond |
|---|---|---|
| Align expectations | Oversee process redesign and other work streams | Review feedback on how changes are working |
| Set the management routines | Manage the governance levers to rebalance power | Track behaviors; recognize positive changes |
| Charter necessary networks and councils | Track progress against the project schedule and take corrective action | Measure business results against new expectations |
| Align designs and missions of each subunit | Manage conflicts that emerge over decision rights and resources; treat them as teaching moments | Begin to plan cross-boundary talent development |
| Set the metrics | Realign reporting systems; ensure that effective data are available | Recheck the operating model; ensure that power is balanced accordingly |
| Finalize decision rights and communicate | Realign budget ownership | |
| Launch work streams | Manage "tipping points" | |
| Manage the staffing process | | |
| Cascade and link new business objectives | | |

**Project Management and Two-Way Communications** →

The agenda for the first executive team launch meeting often sets the work for the next thirty to ninety days in motion. Often new-leader assimilation activities are included in early sessions. The executive team can combine these transition leadership topics with other business items. This is often a time of chaos and uncertainty. A key role for HR is to create "meeting-in-a-box" templates and materials to help middle managers conduct similar launch meetings in their own organization in a cascading fashion. In this way, managers are better prepared to lead their own teams through the change, in alignment with the executive team.

Let's look at the key transition items the executive team needs to oversee during the first thirty to ninety days.

*Align Expectations.*   As a result of the redesign work, there are likely to be some new members on the executive team; roles of existing members may have been altered; or the implementation plan anticipates a shift in responsibilities among members. It is critical to refocus the entire team around the original design criteria and the rationale for the new design. Expectations for what kind of executive group or team they are going to be start here. Each team member's role in the transition process needs to be clear, and the project plan needs to be tested and understood.

*Set the Management Routines.*   Management routines of the new team should be set early in the process, based on the agreed-on executive team charter. Routines will clarify how often the team will meet, what kind of agenda items they will cover, how they will make decisions, and expectations for how they will interact and coordinate between formal meetings. The business dashboard should be set based on the metrics for the new organization. The meeting cadence for the first three months of implementation is likely to be much more frequent than it will be later.

*Charter Necessary Networks and Councils.*   The executive team should identify the networks and councils that need to be chartered and activated to link the organization together. We emphasized in Milestone Three: Integration the power of interactive networks to drive innovation, creativity, and cross-company business-building activities. Well-designed networks need to be a priority in the change process. Clarity of intention, roles, and measures of success is essential to controlling the proliferation of meetings and unnecessary complexity. The senior executives should insist on charters and a clear rationale for these groups to meet, and they should help build excitement around "boundaryless" innovation—largely by acting as role models. The councils and networks then need to create their own routines and use them!

*Align Designs and Missions of Each Subunit.*    Each executive team member may need to realign or completely redesign his or her component of the organization in accordance with the overall design objectives. We encourage each to go through a mini design process—articulating a strategy, developing design criteria, and evaluating a few options—before making any structure, role, or staffing decisions. If the components are complex or the scope of change is large, executive team members may benefit from having a toolkit of templates to guide them through the thought process as well as some facilitation support. The executive team members come back together to share their final detailed designs. It is at this point that the design process moves from a somewhat theoretical activity to one resulting in a very real set of decisions at a granular level. Having the executive team members design and compare their pieces of the organization often surfaces differing assumptions about a whole range of issues.

*Set the Metrics.*    Typically the early design work results in a set of draft metrics for the overall business and major units.

The executive team will usually review these drafts and make significant adjustments. This is an opportunity to ensure alignment across functions. Each executive team member will have a set of individual performance objectives tied to the business goals. Unless the operating model of the organization is that of a true holding company where the executive team members have no interdependence, there should be some joint accountability created through shared metrics. Sharing the sponsorship and success of cross-business processes or projects creates alignment and promotes collaboration in a very real and tangible way.

*Finalize Decision Rights and Communicate.*    Decision rights are among the more useful boundaries suggested by the governance levers model. We have already argued for engaging broad cross sections of people in the decision rights process. Drafts of these documents (such as RACI or similar grids that juxtapose key decisions and the major roles in the business) should have been prepared and reviewed in advance by design team members and subject matter experts. Now the new executive team will work through them in detail and make edits before disseminating them for broad review across functions and deep into the organization. In a matrix organization, it is best to collect feedback on these grids over a thirty-day period and then bring them back to the executive team for another round of review, comments, and edits. Only when these documents have been road tested widely do they begin to gain credibility out in the organization.

Conflicts will often emerge during the early months of implementation. This is when the decision rights are put into action, and each experience should be treated as a learning moment in how to make the matrix work.

*Launch Work Streams.*    As we have seen, the scope of the redesign initiative determines which design elements will be included and then sequenced in the implementation plan. In major design initiatives, such components as process redesign or the creation of a shared service function are assigned to work-stream teams that manage their own detailed project plans. The complexity and lead times on these may vary widely from a few weeks to months. These groups need to be chartered, led, and provided with project management tools. The executive team's role is to ensure that these success factors are in place and to make clear the expected results and time frame.

*Manage the Staffing Process.*   Once the top team is put in place, its members are usually champing at the bit to fill their vacancies—to staff their teams for a fast start. This can create real chaos and certainly doesn't ensure that quality staffing decisions are made. In order to accomplish the kind of staffing excellence we described in Milestone Four: Talent and Leadership—and especially for pivot jobs—the executive team should agree to undertake this work together with some common principles and practices. It starts with an agreement in the top team not to make promises and backroom deals. This is often an early test of trust among the team members.

We have outlined key staffing principles in Milestone Four. The executive team should oversee the process with the clear understanding that going slower so as to get the right people in the right jobs means going much faster later. Even if the operating model for the business doesn't anticipate much integration or talent movement across units, and 95 percent of suggested placements are confirmed by the group, this is a valuable activity. It sets an early norm of looking at talent with an enterprise lens, makes valued and high-potential talent visible to the whole team, and may highlight some opportunities to use new roles as developmental assignments.

*Cascade and Link New Business Objectives.* During the first sixty days or so, it is critical to roll out a set of individual objectives to the extended executive team. Goal alignment is fundamental, particularly if there are changes in strategy that are driving changes in organization. We cannot stress this enough. There is never a better time to cascade goals down through the organization and to link them from side to side than during a significant organization realignment. The case for change, the design criteria, department missions, and role definitions all help define how individual objectives should be linked and aligned across units.

Once the leadership team has identified the key areas of integration and the touch points in the matrix, the actual players in these roles should exchange drafts of objectives, check for alignment, and negotiate mutual support needs. The executive team members are role models for these practices and can facilitate meetings down in their organizations to build these bridges once all the design pieces are in place.

### Months Three to Six: Momentum

Typically after about three months there is a degree of momentum, as confusion gives way to more certainty. The executive team may begin to lose interest in the transition at this point and assume that things are now taking care of themselves. This tendency should be guarded against, and the best way to do that is to make certain there is constant feedback about progress flowing to the executive team. HR leaders out in the organization can take pulse surveys, especially at the key junctures of the matrix.

The management meeting agendas should continue to have placeholders reserved for transition management—at least a few hours every month. Nike's brand president, Charlie Denson, kept organization transition on the monthly meeting agenda for nearly two years as the company managed its shift from a product-based organization to one based on consumer categories in 2006 and 2007. The leaders of several work streams (managing such topics as new reporting systems; large-scale, go-to-market process reengineering; and reskilling of the merchandising community) reported regularly on their progress throughout this period. Problems were solved in real time, and adjustments in the structure, the staffing, and the pace of change were managed continuously. Denson described the organizational shift early in the process as one of the most challenging changes Nike would experience; it turned out to be a model of effective implementation.

Here is a typical list of transition activities that continue to need the attention of the executive team during the three- to six-month momentum phase:

- Continue to oversee process redesign and other work streams
- Manage the governance levers to rebalance power
- Track progress against the project schedule and take corrective action
- Manage conflicts that emerge over decision rights and resources
- Realign reporting systems—ensure that effective data are available
- Realign budget ownership
- Manage tipping points (see the section "Tipping Points" in this chapter)

### *Months Six to Twelve (and Beyond): Learning and Adjusting*

In the later phases of implementation, the frequency of progress reviews will slow, but the discipline should not waver. If major blocks of design work were staged for later implementation, these are likely to need management support at specific points in time. The rollout of a new shared service unit or the activation of a major new business process are examples. Often end-to-end redesign of support functions (for example, finance, IT, or HR) begins at this stage in a major company-wide transition. The executive team should be holding these groups accountable to be certain they are designing themselves against a common framework; and executive leadership will need to support change inside the operating units as the new functional designs are implemented.

Executives need to be in the field listening and bringing feedback to the leader and their colleagues during this phase. Internal organization development and HR staff need to do their own diagnostic work and bring objective data forward with ideas for enhancing performance.

Six to twelve months into the transition is about the right time to gather data to find early indicators that the organizational realignments are creating the expected capabilities. Leaders also need to pay attention to the emotions of people who view themselves as losing status and influence in restructurings. Even as it is important for people to understand the business case for change, it is equally important to engage them emotionally in building a new understanding of their contribution. If the change is perceived as a negation of the hard work of people who made the business successful in the past, there will be natural resistance. IBM's historic transformation in the 1990s was driven by many strategic events. But it worked because the company was able to transform its identity from being a global team of people who built great computers to one that solved difficult business problems. ("Making the Emotional Case for Change," 2010).

A major part of the transition phase is helping individual employees understand how their identity is changing and what they need to do to be successful in the new environment. In the case of an organizational restructuring, this is most important for the people in the legacy units who may in fact be giving up power and influence in the future state.

Here are the items likely to remain on the executive agenda during the learning and adjusting phase:

- Engage employees and ask for honest feedback on how the changes are working
- Track behaviors—recognize and celebrate positive changes
- Measure business results against new expectations
- Begin to plan cross-boundary talent development
- Recheck the operating model and ensure that power is balanced accordingly

## TIPPING POINTS

We recently worked with a consumer products company that established a handful of global customer units to bring the voice of a few very powerful retailers into the entire business process, from new product creation to marketing and supply chain management. A set of formal decision rights was established, and the new executives were placed on key business teams. But more than a year into the transition, the chief executive was disappointed at the impact these positions were having in the decision-making process.

Walmart and Carrefour insisted on more responsiveness than the consumer products company was showing in its ability to create differentiated product for their shoppers. Shortly after a particularly heated meeting with a customer, the chief executive, with a stroke of a pen, made a move that became a *tipping point*—a change in power that shifts the company's momentum in a new direction. He transferred a set of core budget line items from the very powerful product divisions over to the customer units. The symbolism of the move in this culture was seismic.

We have discovered in working with our clients that tipping points are a powerful way for the executive team to navigate an organizational transition. Tipping points, in the context of organization change, are tangible actions or decisions that are read by the organization as evidence that something very different is happening. They are symbolic actions because they have a disproportionate impact in altering power dynamics. They send signals, but they are quite concrete. Often they disturb sacred cows. A series of tipping points can be shrewdly plotted on a long- or short-horizon Gantt chart to be triggered at just the right time as part of a steady-rolling transition from here to the future state. And tipping points can be delayed or triggered sooner based on the impact of preceding events. In this way they are a potent set of tools for executives to guide, cajole, and course-correct their way through the transition plan. They are especially useful in balancing matrix relationships.

Tipping points that give greater decision power and influence to a given unit or function are best activated when it is clear that the unit has the know-how and capabilities to put that power to work to benefit the business. Tipping points should also be measured against and informed by external events. As an example, when a new business unit begins to develop more global products that gain traction in local markets, then product development power and resources can be taken away from the local geographic units. The diagnostic measures suggested by the governance levers model are used to measure results and guide tipping points.

The example in the previous chapter of the medical products company that set a two-year destination for its transition illustrates the use of tipping points, as shown in Figure 14.2.

FIGURE 14.2. *Future State Organization for Medical Products Company*

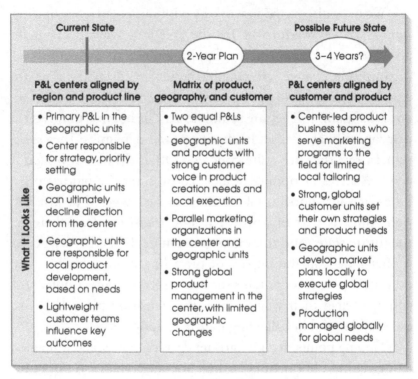

Although the business was strong and successful, the executive team anticipated the need to shift strategy and organization to focus more on future sources of growth. Global customers were demanding more cross-border coordination and bundled solutions, rather than stand-alone products. Salespeople in the regions and product lines were competing internally. Power in the matrix needed to shift from dominant regions, with weaker product divisions and even weaker customer teams, to powerful customer teams partnered with the same product divisions and more narrowly empowered regions.

The executive team also recognized that this represented a major change for a company that had long operated with a culture and reward system that favored local responsiveness over global cooperation. Leadership communicated that changes in structure were likely at some point. But a series of discussions over many months concluded that a big-bang shift was too risky, especially in relation to the distribution channels.

An implementation plan laid out a series of actions, starting with establishment of a set of powerful customer management roles. Leadership would realign decision making, metrics, rewards, and governance over a period of time. Tipping points were a key part of the transition at the medical products company. Here are some of the highlights of those tipping points in the sequence in which they were triggered, once the new global leaders were put in place:

- Small global sales teams are established in the home regions of major customers; global leaders make the appointments with regional input (month two).

- Global account managers are at the table, sitting on regional executive teams (month three).

- Product design decisions are made across product units with a strong voice-of-the-customer process (month five).

- Increased control of expense resources is given to the global customer teams (training, travel, and so on) (month six, as new budget year begins).

- Talent reviews begin to move key talent from regional to global roles (month nine).

- Global account leaders are given veto rights in staffing of all sales and marketing roles in regions (month twelve).

- Fifty percent of products delivered in-region are drawn from global offerings (month eighteen).

One of the most powerful tipping points you can use in an organization redesign that shifts focus and power is to move a heavyweight player from the traditional business into a newly minted position tied to the future state. This is a big event that sends big signals. Several times we have watched the managers of internal start-ups struggle to hold their own in the fight for resources against their well-heeled peers who run large legacy organizations. Only when a highly regarded executive from the legacy business was placed into the start-up role did conversation at the executive team's table begin to change.

# Milestone Five Summary: Transition

*Chapter Thirteen: Set the Implementation Plan*

- Implementation planning starts with a clear destination—a summary statement of the future state. Even in complex transitions that may include several phases, it is important to define the longer-term state even if it is an approximation that may change.

- Pacing of the transition needs to be defined. An evolutionary approach can be effective if the pressure for change is not urgent. But when a clear change of strategy has occurred or when significant changes in the external environment are apparent, a faster change may be necessary. In these cases, delays only tend to make progress more difficult.

- A project plan is needed for the implementation to be managed with energy and discipline. Sequencing the major steps in the process is essential. Key guideposts in the project plan will include structure shifts, business process changes, realignment of reporting systems, and development of new skills. The sequence in which these changes take place should build the needed capabilities in a logical order and reflect the organization's capacity for change.

*Chapter Fourteen: Navigate the Transition*

- Most major implementation projects can be broken into three time frames:
  - Launch—the first ninety days
  - Momentum—months three to six
  - Learning and adjusting—months six to twelve (and beyond)

- In the launch stage, the leadership team must be engaged and very visible. A key element of the launch is gaining full alignment regarding how they will manage the new organization and how they will operate as an executive team. New management routines should be established at the kick-off. Staffing the new organization will occur largely during this stage. Executives will also create networks and councils, set decision rights, and launch work streams focused on specific design tasks.

- Over the next three to twelve months and beyond, the leadership team will manage the project plan. Typical transition tasks include process redesign, overseeing power allocation through effective governance, managing conflicts, realigning budgets and reporting systems, and tracking behaviors. The intent of the new organizational arrangements should not being subverted by old norms.

- The leadership team should find a few very tangible tipping points (changes in practice or power allocation) that will have a disproportionately large impact in demonstrating that the change initiative is really happening. Examples of tipping points are a transfer of budget ownership or the placement of a high-powered executive in a new role.

# CONCLUSION

## Organization Design in Action

Making an organization design change is not a one-time decision. It is a process of generating and evaluating alternatives in relation to a set of criteria. It is complicated by the need to involve people with divergent perspectives who must come together to design something that they can't see. Yet the decisions that are made about the organization will impact jobs and careers, status and power—of both the organization's leaders and the employees who place trust in them to make well-considered choices. Company history and politics can easily distort efforts to run a structured, objective decision-making process.

Organization design is best thought of as a project that requires the same tools, attention, and resources as any other significant business change or investment. In this part of the book we look at organization design through the lens of the process of design—how to manage and lead the organization design project to achieve the five milestones.

*The Five Milestone Design Process*

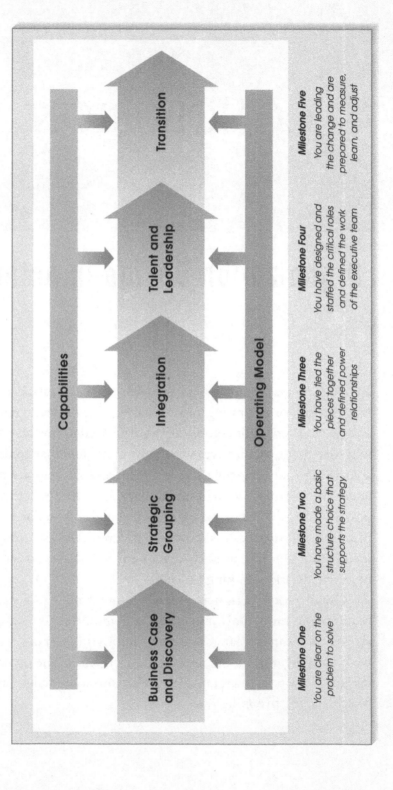

Capabilities

Operating Model

Business Case and Discovery

Strategic Grouping

Integration

Talent and Leadership

Transition

**Milestone One**
*You are clear on the problem to solve*

**Milestone Two**
*You have made a basic structure choice that supports the strategy*

**Milestone Three**
*You have tied the pieces together and defined power relationships*

**Milestone Four**
*You have designed and staffed the critical roles and defined the work of the executive team*

**Milestone Five**
*You are leading the change and are prepared to measure, learn, and adjust*

Although every project will have its own particular flow, we have found that there is a general set of steps that each design project incorporates. The five milestone process that we have used throughout the book lays these out at a high level. In Chapter Fifteen, we offer guidelines to determine who participates at various stages, how to get the most from their involvement, and how to keep the project tied to an overall timeline.

We strongly believe that involving a broad range of perspectives in the design process enriches the quality of decisions that are made and makes the work of transition and implementation easier. We also recognize that many leaders and HR professionals are uncomfortable with the potential loss of control and potential for distraction that bringing together large groups of people can represent. In Chapter Sixteen we share, in detail, how to plan and facilitate a successful large-group design session—what we call a *charette*—to accelerate design decision making. It isn't always the right approach, but it's one that executives and organization design experts should know how to use.

This part of the book concludes with a thought for business and organization leaders who are embarking on an organization design project. We summarize why we believe so strongly that organization design is an essential competence for any leader and discuss how to enhance this competence to increase your personal effectiveness in building great organizations.

# Roles, Involvement, and the Project Timeline

In this chapter, we highlight

- Key roles needed to guide the organization design project
- Options for involvement
- A basic project timeline of key activities within the five milestone process
- Some approaches for building an internal organization design capability, with a summary of the internal consulting skills and competencies required

## KEY ROLES

The organization design project benefits from clear roles for the leaders, the design team members, and the staff and consulting experts who support the initiative. It helps to use nomenclature that everyone understands the same way.

## Leader

The leader is the person in the senior-most position of the organizational unit to be redesigned. The leader makes the organization design decisions. All work that is conducted as part of the project is *input* to this leader. The leader is the client for the work.

## Sponsor

The sponsor has a direct interest in the organization and is usually the leader's manager. If the leader is the CEO, the sponsor and leader may be one and the same, or the sponsor may be a committee of the board. This role may provide the budget and resources for the project. The sponsor may or may not choose to provide input into the design options. The sponsor should not be able to veto the design. Rather, it is better to have the sponsor lay out from the beginning any boundaries or criteria that must be adhered to if the leader's organization is nested within a larger whole. In this way, the leader is empowered to make final design decisions knowing they are in alignment with the sponsor and will be supported.

## Executive Team

The executive team consists of the current direct reports to the leader. In a given organization, this group may be called the leadership team, the management team, senior staff, or some other term. The executive team works closely with the leader to set the strategy and the design criteria. Because members of this group often have a vested interest in maintaining power and their current roles, the actual design work should include a broader group of managers at levels below to ensure that the status quo does not become the preferred option.

### Human Resources

The head of human resources or the HR business partner for the unit often acts as the internal coach on organization design. Even if the HR partner is not a deep expert in organization design, he or she needs to understand the major milestones and principles, and how best to structure the project to be effective. The HR partner coaches the leader on what makes for an effective process, whom to involve at each step, and the talent implications of options under consideration. If a member of the executive team, HR should also be an active participant in generating options and contributing to content discussions. HR should not be side-lined solely into a project management or facilitation role.

### Organization Development and Effectiveness

This role is typically filled by a corporate resource or an external consultant. If the HR leader is not familiar with the organization design process, the OD professional often assists with that. The OD professional can also facilitate meetings, allowing the HR executive to focus on contributing to the discussion, rather than running the process. The O D role often also includes bringing the tools, external examples, and organization design models needed to inform and stimulate design work. It may also be helpful to have the person in this role conduct the assessment in order to supply objective data and feedback.

### Core Team

The core team (sometimes called the steering committee) makes process decisions throughout the project (scheduling, involvement, review of materials, and management of external consultants). The core team is typically composed of the leader, human resources, organization development, and the head of finance or strategy.

By involving strategy, the organization design work becomes a strategy implementation project, and the links between the two are tight. Occasionally an operating leader will be added to make certain that the team is well anchored to the business.

## Involving the Right People in the Process

We strongly believe that involving a broad range of perspectives in the design process—from the assessment to the generation and evaluation of alternatives—enriches the quality of decisions that are made and eases the tasks of transition and implementation. There are situations, however, where limiting participation is appropriate. Let's review four different ways to involve people in the design process, ranging from including very limited numbers of people, in a generally secretive approach, to much broader engagement.

### The Expert Model

In the expert model, the leader works with a very small group of advisers and an internal or external consultant. Even the executive team may not be aware of the work. Experts may interview a small number of top players and develop a few design concepts. They share design options with the leader, who may then seek reactions from some trusted team members or colleagues. The leader makes a decision and carefully orchestrates a communication plan to launch the change. This approach is appropriate if the redesign will result in a significant downsizing and the leader knows that certain segments of the organization will be closed down or sold off. In other situations, there may be a number of members of the executive team who will be replaced. In these cases, it is appropriate to decide on and take these actions before involving more people in designing the new organization.

Leaders are, however, often drawn to this approach even in circumstances that don't require limiting participation. It feels cleaner and less disruptive. The thinking is, "We'll figure out the change without distracting people from delivering today's work. By keeping the group small and the process quiet, we'll avoid rumors and anxiety." The problem with this approach is not related to the design decisions. The leader may come up with quite sound ideas, although we do find that greater participation usually does result in better ideas. The larger problem is that without some open involvement and debate early on, implementation is slowed. The rest of the executive team and broader management corps will have to go through the same thought process as the leader, explore and reject options, and understand the rationale behind the end result. Any time saved by keeping the design process contained is lost in a longer and more complex change management task.

### Executive Team as Design Team

Here, the executive team works closely with the leader to develop and evaluate options. If significant change is envisioned and the competence level is not high at levels below, it may make sense to limit initial design involvement to the executive team. This approach is successful when the executive team works well together and decisions need to be made quickly. After the leader makes high-level design choices in close consultation with the executive team, a broader group of employees can be brought in to detail the design and participate in implementation.

An executive team may advocate for this approach, and it can be effective, but it has some drawbacks. Because the group that reports directly to the leader is often the most insecure in the design process—their past success is no longer what is needed for the future, and at least some of their roles or power bases are likely to shift—we find that the executive team members tend to defend the status quo. In our experience, the members of the executive team tend to see issues only with other parts of the organization, rarely their own; and their point of view is, naturally, influenced by the impact each change option may have on their personal ambitions. An outside consultant can play a catalyst role, challenging the thinking of the group, but only if the consultant is quite assertive and willing to offend stakeholders, and the top leader welcomes that role.

### Delegated Design Team

In this approach, the executive team identifies a small group of high-potential employees two or three levels down and assigns them the task of exploring design options. The design team presents back a set of alternatives and a recommendation to the leadership team. This design approach has the appeal of an action-learning developmental experience for the staff involved. It broadens the perspectives on the issues.

We usually find that these design teams do excellent work as long as they have been supported with assertive, effective organization design expertise, some project management help, and exposure to some outside thinking on the business environment and best practices. They often become very tightly knit teams as a result of participating together in what becomes a substantial learning event.

A problem with a delegated design team is that the executive team doesn't own the process or options. If the executive team is allowed only to review proposed options, rather than to fully participate in developing and owning them, they tend to default to the most conservative alternative, as they have not been part of the learning process. We've seen many design teams who worked hard to come up with an honest and creative recommendation and were then frustrated to find themselves in the middle of a turf war. With this approach, the leader can end up with a list of arguments for what won't work, rather than a process that builds momentum toward a new future.

### Multilevel Design Team

We find that a multilevel design team that mixes members of the executive team and managers at two or three levels below results in the best input and overcomes the problems posed by the aforementioned options. A multilevel design team may comprise a handful of people who are viewed as thought leaders in the business, and who are personally involved in most or all design tasks. Or the team may be a quite large group who participate more periodically by bringing very diverse perspectives and creativity into the process early on, followed by targeted involvement in smaller work-stream teams later in the design process. This large-group approach can be quite effective; it includes a high-involvement event that we call the design charette, which we will describe in detail in the next chapter.

In the multilevel design process, employees three or four levels below the leader will be provided with strategy and assessment data and will likely be talking with colleagues about the process and ideas that are emerging. With this approach, the design work cannot be kept a secret. It should be used with projects focused on growth, innovation, and improving effectiveness, where the energy and ideas of a broader set of employees can be harnessed and used. It is not appropriate if these employees will be asked to significantly downsize the organization or eliminate whole components.

## Project Timeline

In many ways, an organization design project follows the same arc whether for a whole company of thirty thousand or a thirty-person staff function. Clearly the scope and complexity of issues are much greater in the former, and the implementation phase will certainly be longer as well. However, the core steps of clarifying the business case, determining the basic framework, and making top-level staffing decisions are the same for each. Table 15.1 outlines a typical project plan, offered not as a recipe to follow but as a general guide.

## Building Organization Design Capability

Although there is debate about where organization design should reside within a firm, today it is most often an HR offering. Many human resources organizations have realigned their service delivery models in order to concentrate know-how such as organization design and development into small, higher-powered centers of expertise. At the same time, most companies have worked to refocus the HR generalists into business partner roles that pull organization and talent tools into the operating units. New technology platforms, shared service centers, and outsourcing have freed up significant amounts of time, and have raised expectations that the function will contribute more to business decisions about organization and talent. The good news is that business leaders are looking to their internal human resource partners to provide guidance and tools that will provide true competitive advantage. The challenge is not to rely on only a few specialists but to create a shared capability across the HR function. To do this requires investments in methodology and

TABLE 15.1. *Typical Project Plan*

| Action and Outcome | Notes | Typical Elapsed Time |
|---|---|---|
| **BUSINESS CASE AND DISCOVERY** | | |
| **Strategy Clarification** The strategy is clear and the executive team agrees with it and supports it. | Because organization design often follows a strategy change, this may be quite clear and take no time at all. However, there may be a need to gather data or to gain agreement among the executive team on the company's future direction. | No time to one month |
| **Assessment** The current-state baseline is understood (misalignments as well as strengths to leverage). | Typically 12–25 interviews and a few focus groups often provide enough information if the participants are well selected to sample the organization. The assessment also includes a review of other data (organization charts; strategy documents; financial, customer, employee, competitor, and industry data). The full assessment report is usually reviewed with the leader first and then the executive team. An edited version is then produced to be shared with the broader organization. | Three to six weeks to schedule and conduct interviews and focus groups One to two weeks to assess data and produce a findings report |

**Design Criteria**

The executive team has agreed on the capabilities the new organization must have, against which all options will be tested.

Design criteria are developed by the executive team after they have reviewed the assessment findings.

Two approaches can be used. In the first, the executive team reaches full agreement on a short list of three to seven capabilities. These are then given to the design team to use. In the second, the executive team narrows the list to about a dozen. The design team then has the opportunity to work with and select the most critical.

One week

## STRATEGIC GROUPING AND INTEGRATION

**Generating Options**

A series of options that meet the design criteria are developed and evaluated using a charette.

A design charette should be considered here. The leader can take three approaches:

1. He may provide the design team with the design criteria and a blank slate in order to elicit the broadest range of ideas.

2. He may provide the group with a predetermined set of options in order to focus and direct the work.

3. He may make top-level framework decisions (for example, restructuring the executive team) and then engage the design team in developing the design concept in more detail, including integrating mechanisms.

Three to six weeks

The charette must be designed, prework sent out, and presenters prepared.

The extra time is needed if two charettes are used: one to develop and narrow options, and another to develop more design detail.

*(Continued)*

TABLE 15.1. (*Continued*)

| Action and Outcome | Notes | Typical Elapsed Time |
|---|---|---|
| **Selection of the Best Design Option**<br>The leader makes decisions about the new design—high-level structure, new roles, key integration points. | The advantage of the charette process is that a number of core ideas usually emerge that the leader can build on. If the leader's organization is nested in a larger organization, the leader may choose at this time to meet with peers, internal customers, and the sponsor to get feedback on the preferred option before making a final decision. | Two to six weeks |
| **Design Details**<br>The design is detailed to the level that staffing decisions can be made. | Once the framework is set, there will still be much design work to carry out depending on the complexity of the organization and the scope of the change. Work-stream teams—populated by participants from the charette and led by members of the executive team—develop the details of what needs to change. This may include process redesign, decision rights, new role definitions, customer interface, metric realignment, and so on. | One to three months<br>(This work comes back to the new executive team for approval, and therefore the timing is tightly linked to the next step.) |

## TALENT AND LEADERSHIP

**Executive Team Staffing**
The direct report structure is in place and all roles have been defined and filled.

This step often precedes or occurs concurrently with the detailed design work. Some roles may be left open for some time if an outside hire is sought.

One week to months

**Organization Staffing**
All critical roles have been filled; a process for making any talent moves has been defined and communicated, and is under way

Once the executive team is in place, members can begin making role and staffing decisions within their units in accordance with the design framework and detailed design work that is under way or completed.

For the direct reports to the executive team and critical "pivot point" roles, staffing changes should be reviewed by the leader and the executive team together to ensure that the talent is managed with an enterprise view.

One to several months

## TRANSITION

**Implementation**
The organization is operating in accordance with the new design.

Implementation begins when the majority of designing and planning is complete and people begin to transition to their new roles. This may occur gradually, or there may be a "go live" date to kick off this phase. Employees build the capabilities to execute successfully against the strategy.

Three months to two years

skill building as well as an understanding of what makes for an excellent organization design practitioner.

### Methodology

This includes an agreed-to, common set of *concepts and principles* that guide HR and the business when making design decisions; a straightforward and well-understood *process* that ensures sound decisions, a disciplined approach, and the right involvement and governance at each step; and a customized and easy-to-use set of *tools* perceived by managers as beneficial to decision making and implementation.

### Skilled HR and OD Staff

The individuals tasked with guiding the organization design process need a solid understanding of the methodology, concepts, and tools that will be used in the company; mechanisms to maintain methodology, share best practices, and foster continued learning within the community of practice; and clear roles and responsibilities for initiating and carrying out design projects.

The goal is to build a capability that enables the HR team to work consistently and seamlessly together across client groups, and all clients to experience confident and capable HR staff regardless of who is assisting them. We find that a three-part approach works well.

The first is to select an organization design methodology and provide a training program in the fundamentals for the HR team. This ensures a common base of knowledge, shared experience, and practice using the tools, and agreement on internal roles and operating procedures.

Second, cross-business teams of HR staff work on organization design projects together. The projects can be led by an internal organization design expert or an external consultant. The team helps with the assessment, facilitates small groups at the charette, and supports work-stream teams as they detail the design. At each step there is real-time learning, reflection, and coaching.

The third step in building an internal capability is to select those who have a deep interest and aptitude for the work and invest in advanced practitioner training for them or attendance at organization design conferences. These "black belts" can emerge from the organization development team, from among the business partners, from the leadership development group, or from other HR disciplines.

### *Organization Design Consulting Skills*

Design is both an analytical and creative process. The analytical elements are reflected in the strategy, performance data, and decision frameworks that are used. But organization design is also a creative, integrative activity based on an understanding of patterns of organizational behavior. Good organization design embodies the same values found in the design of more common objects: balance, proportion, and unity. The key difference between organization and industrial design is that the organization is an invisible yet powerful construct that shapes the web of work relationships rather than a tangible object.

Design thinking is a blend of art and science—intuition and analytics. It balances the natural tensions of reliability (producing consistent, predictable outcomes) with validity (producing outcomes that meet a desired objective) (Martin, 2009). Tim Brown, CEO of the design firm IDEO, ranked one of the ten most innovative companies in the world, observes, "The company 're-org' . . . is one of the most fateful and complex design problems any company may face, though it is rarely accompanied by any of the characteristics of good design thinking. Meetings are called in which there is no brainstorming; organizational charts are drawn up with little evidence of any thinking with the hands; plans are made and directives are issued without the benefit of prototyping" (Brown, 2009, p. 102).

The skilled organization design consultant—whether internal or external—brings design thinking to the process. The field of organization design has matured and coalesced since the mid-1990s. Designers can draw on a robust set of readily available models, tools, guides, and methodologies. But, as in any field, knowledge is not enough. Organization design requires a particular set of competencies and skills (Kates, 2010).

*Diagnostic and Analytic Skills.*   The organization designer must have the ability to ask the right questions and make sense of the answers. Like a physician who sorts through symptoms that may have many causes and determines the correct underlying disease, the organization designer has to be able to determine the root causes of performance issues in the system. The designer then analyzes what changes will have the most impact and the greatest likelihood of success in this particular context.

*Deep Curiosity About Organizations as Systems.*   Effective organization design consultants are fascinated by the complexity of business and organizational life. They like to solve multifaceted problems and do not stop at easy answers or one-dimensional solutions. It is important to be able see an organization as more than a collection of individuals and to be able to discern the interconnected political, social, and information networks that have formed. Organization designers tend to be wide ranging in their personal interests, well read on a broad range of topics, and inquisitive about how things work below the surface.

*Design Mind-Set.* Designers—whether of organizations, buildings, IT systems, or functional objects—share a common ability to conceive of and articulate how their designs will work. They take problems and reframe them. Designers ask the right questions, generate a wide range of options, and guide the selection of the best solution. They know that the process is rarely linear but iterative, and enhanced by contributions from different perspectives. Designers are often ambidextrous thinkers, comfortable with solving for both the possible and the practical.

*Pattern Recognition.*  Organization design is not for the neophyte. One must have enough hands-on, personal experience working with a variety of organizations to build the expertise to recognize and sort patterns. Although one can become familiar with frameworks from training programs and reading, pattern recognition cannot come from a book. It grows from experience and structured reflection that turns data into wisdom. Organization design is typically a field that one comes to from another, because the discipline rests on so many different pillars of analysis.

*Consulting and Facilitation Skills.*  Successful organization design requires a high level of confidence and competence to guide leadership teams through a design process, which is another reason why organization design is a field for the seasoned professional. All the core consulting skills—in contracting, assessment, facilitation, written communication, and presentation—are used in the organization design process. One has to be comfortable with surfacing and managing conflict, because the core of design is to debate options and differences before choosing a solution. The designer must be comfortable facilitating senior groups through a creative and sometimes emotional or contentious process.

In any design meeting, there will be those who are most comfortable with building on the past, leveraging strengths, and seeking the proven route that others have traveled before. Other participants will want to put their energy into big ideas that are novel and energizing. Helping both of these ends of the spectrum have a productive dialogue and create something new together is the facilitator's role. Although the leader and her team have to discover and own the solution themselves, the designer is there to educate them about the realities and possibilities, provide them the language and tools to make decisions, and challenge and guide them to implementable solutions.

# The Design Charette

THE MOST IMPORTANT POINT IN THE FIVE MILESTONE process where a diverse group needs to think both analytically and creatively is at the strategic grouping phase. It is at this phase that the framework for the future organization is set. Once these structural choices are made, subsequent design choices are narrowed and alternative paths are closed. Therefore, at this stage the leader should want to ensure that he or she is considering the widest range of options before committing to a preferred direction. This is the time to encourage divergent and inventive thinking. A radical option may have elements that can be incorporated into a more pragmatic solution, or may represent a possible long-term future state.

Design is a type of innovation. As with other types of creative processes, the people who identify a problem may not be the best ones to solve it. In addition, creative thinking often occurs at the intersection of disciplines, when diverse perspectives come together.

We have experimented with many ways to foster innovate thinking and problem solving. We have found that a *design charette* is the most effective vehicle to quickly focus a diverse group on a design problem and to generate and evaluate a range of options.

In this chapter, we

- Define a charette, suggest who should participate, provide guidance on clarifying the decision authority, and share a detailed agenda and facilitation tips
- Suggest the use of a transition leader role to guide implementation
- Offer some measures of success for the organization design project

## DEFINITION OF A CHARETTE

A design charette is a multiday, highly structured and facilitated working session. The term is borrowed from the architecture field and refers to a collaborative session where a group drafts a solution to a design problem.* An organization design charette has two defining aspects:

1. *Whole system in the room.* The design charette uses large-group methodology to bring together representatives from

---

* The word *charette* is thought to originate from the nineteenth-century French word for "cart." It was not unknown for student architects to continue working up to the last minute on the illustrations for their design presentations, even while riding in the school cart ("en charette") through the streets of Paris en route to submitting the projects to their professors. Hence the current design-related usage in conjunction with working intensely on design options. In addition, in the sixteenth, seventeenth, and eighteenth centuries, when travel took long periods, a charette referred to the long carriage rides in which politicians and policymakers would be sequestered together and would frequently collaborate to solve a set of problems over the duration of their journey. From this meaning we draw the collaborative aspect of the term.

as much of a complete system as possible to work holistically on a business issue (Axelrod, 2002). Group size is anywhere from twelve to more than a hundred people.

2. *Intensive and iterative.* The charette typically takes place over two or more days and away from the office, if possible. The work is rigorous, with iterations of small groups working in parallel and then coming together to review, evaluate, and revise.

## WHO SHOULD PARTICIPATE IN THE CHARETTE?

The number and composition of participants in the charette will be different for every organization. If the unit is small, you may be able to have nearly everyone come. If you are redesigning a unit or company of thousands, then representatives have to be carefully selected both to provide the needed diversity of input and to give face validity to the recommendations in the view of those who are not there. The goal is to have a participant list that anyone in the organization could look at and say, "My part of the organization was represented, and I can trust this group." Use the following list as a start:

- Leader
- Executive team (direct reports to the leader must be there)
- Assessment participants, or some subset
- Representatives of various functions and geographic units
- Both line and staff (be sure there is the right balance)
- Variety of levels
- Skeptics as well as positive influencers

- Long-tenured employees who represent the history of the organization, as well as those who are new and have worked in companies with different models
- Stakeholders—internal and external customers, suppliers, partners

We prefer to have a minimum of twenty-five participants to provide the range of perspectives as well as the energy that this type of work demands. Our groups range up to one hundred in size, but others have used similar techniques effectively with groups of five hundred (Axelrod, 2002). The process is basically the same, with only the number of facilitators and administrative support staff needing to be scaled.

## DECISION PROCESS

Design decisions are a leader's prerogative and responsibility. They cannot be delegated. The charette is not a forum to make collective decisions. It is a mechanism to provide thoughtful input to the leader so that he or she can make well-considered, sound, and defensible changes to the organization. Clarity on these expectations is critical.

It is a mistake to allow participants to believe that they are coming together to reach a consensus on the future of the organization. Consensus means everyone agrees. To reach that point on such a complex topic means that some people will have vetoes and others will compromise their views.

Instead, the goal of a charette is creativity and collaborative learning; in the ideal outcome, the group has generated new options that no one in the room walked in with. We find that groups which understand clearly that their work is to provide input and that the leader will make the final decisions actually feel freer to be fully creative. They are no longer constrained by the need to worry about how suggestions might affect others in the room.

The reality is that the charette process almost always yields a set of core ideas around which the participants, no matter how diverse, come together. But that is not the goal. In all communication and invitations, make sure that participants understand that the charette is about generating ideas, input, and options, and that decisions will be made later.

## CHARETTE PLAN

The charette is the first meeting of the new organization—even though the new organization hasn't even been designed! The tone of the charette itself signals a fresh way of working for many organizations. The process models how to solve a complex business problem collaboratively across organizational borders that may have represented boundaries in the past. The quality of planning and preparation for the charette is as important as the facilitation.

We have found two days to be the right length of time. Two days provide a group with enough time to take the work of generating and evaluating options to a place where the leader needs to make a decision. Less time feels rushed, and more time rarely adds value, as the group can get only so far before a major decision point is reached. The two-day agenda breaks into four segments, as shown in the following list. Each element of the agenda is described in the next sections.

*High-Level View of the Design Charette Agenda*
First morning: Creating a common understanding
    Welcome
    Assessment feedback

Strategy and data
Design criteria
Models
First afternoon: Generating options
Starting point and parameters
Design generation
Sharing
Second morning: Reviewing, revising, detailing
Review
Detailed design
Sharing and evaluation
Second afternoon: Planning and communication
Work streams
Next steps
Communication

### Pre-Charette Assignment

The participants should come prepared to work and create together. Send customer, financial, performance, and competitor data ahead of time so that everyone is grounded in the facts. Find a case study or article that is relevant to the central design dilemma (for example, innovation, global expansion, moving from a product to solutions strategy) to stimulate thinking. In addition, send a reading assignment that provides an overview of organization design concepts so that the group arrives with a common language and set of design tools.

### First Morning: Creating a Common Understanding

The objective of the first morning is to bring everyone in the room to the same point of knowledge. If you truly are involving a diverse group, then they will be coming not just with different views but with different levels of background information, understanding of the situation, and assumptions about what others think. Laying this groundwork is the foundation of a successful charette.

*Welcome.*   The leader starts off the session with a welcome and a clear statement of the objectives for the two days and the decision process. If the group has not worked together before and people do not know each other well, you may want to start the evening before with a dinner and a warm-up activity to facilitate introductions.

*Assessment Feedback.*   The next step is to feed back the assessment findings and create shared understanding of the problem statement. The feedback should be presented by whoever conducted the assessment, usually either the internal or external consultant. The feedback from interviews and focus groups is presented in summary form. The goal is to put the issues on the table in a direct and honest way, but not to make public any information that is so negative about one part of the organization that it makes productive teamwork difficult. Leaders may resist sharing the assessment feedback, giving such reasons as, "We should focus on the future," "Why stir up bad feelings about what doesn't work?" "Everyone knows what the problems are . . ." We often do find through our assessment work that there is strong convergence on the definition of the problem. However, the participants in the room do not know this. By ensuring that "everyone knows what everyone knows" we are able to reduce a lot of the tension that can surround the design process. By presenting the issues and spending about an hour allowing table groups to discuss the findings together, identify themes, and ask questions, we are able to put the past aside and focus the group on building a future together. If we skip this important step, the issues will often surface throughout the two days in an unhealthy and unproductive way.

*Strategy and Data.*   The leader or members of the leadership team presents the key elements of the strategy and highlights relevant customer, financial, performance, and competitor data. Even if everyone has heard this presentation before, they may not have heard it all at the same time or in this context. Allow time for answering questions of clarity.

*Design Criteria.*   Following discussion of the strategy, we present the group with a draft list of design criteria. These have either been summarized from the assessment in response to a question regarding what capabilities the new organization needs, or developed by the executive team. We like to present the group with a handout that has a list of eight to twelve potential criteria and ask each person to circle (and edit if desired) the five most important. The handouts are collected and summarized, and a refined list of criteria is distributed before the design work in the afternoon. It is again reviewed and refined at the end of the day or the beginning of the second day. If the executive team has already narrowed and refined the list before the charette, then the task can be for the group to rank-order the criteria. Ranking by importance will help the group focus on trade-offs and sequencing. It is important that the participants do some refining or ranking activity with the criteria so that the criteria are discussed and owned by the full group.

*Models.*   We finish the morning with an educational session; we present a few models to stimulate participants' thinking and reactions. These may include examples of the organization design approaches of other companies, inside or outside the industry. Although we don't believe that benchmarking is the only way to inform design decisions, it can be useful in disturbing established thinking.

The core team can also present straw models for how the organization might be redesigned. These models should represent a spectrum of options; they should not be presented as recommendations but rather as a way to stimulate initial discussion and debate.

### First Afternoon: Generating Options

The first afternoon is typically spent in small groups to generate options and then in a large forum to share and identify ideas to carry forward.

***Starting Point and Parameters.***   To ensure that the small groups are clear about the task, it is important to define expected deliverables, as well as assumptions or parameters. There are three general starting points:

- *Blank slate.* The leader wants the group to generate framework options without any constraints except that the option should meet the design criteria. This approach gives the most freedom to the group and ensures that they generate a broad range of ideas.
- *Test and refine.* The leader has a preferred framework option but is open to change. The leader presents his or her thought process that led to the preferred alternative as well as other options considered. The group uses the framework as a starting point but is not limited by it.
- *Make it work.* The leader has already determined the framework and high-level strategic grouping, and a new executive team may already be in place. The charette participants are charged with generating options for how the components will work together. This is commonly used if there are clear executive team or framework changes to be

made and the participants' time is best spent on the next level of design.

The leader should clearly state the scope of change and any nonnegotiable parameters. This is also the time to be honest about job security. If the redesign is part of a growth strategy, then the leader can reassure the group that the work is not focused on job elimination. If he or she can say no one will lose a job, that message is ideal. However, growth often means repositioning resources and funding new investments by creating smaller and more efficient core activities. If this is the case, the leader should be honest that some jobs may disappear and that there may not be roles in the new organization that fit the skills of the current workforce and managers.

*Design Generation.*    For the small-group work, teams of five to seven are ideal. If you don't have a large number of participants, it's better to use groups of three and have more groups working. For example, if you have only twelve people at the charette, make four trios, rather than two groups of six. Mix the composition of the groups, ensuring a microcosm of the organization in each, with both subject matter knowledge and an outside perspective represented in the groups where possible.

With the *blank slate* approach, it is best to have all the groups focused on the same task so that a number of options can be compared. For the *test and refine* or *make it work* starting points, you may want to assign groups different parts of the organization on which to focus.

Typical instructions to the groups include the following:

- Create a picture of the organization 18 (or 24 or 36) months from now.
- Pay attention to the design criteria.

- The purpose of this round is to generate options and ideas; it is not necessarily to agree or try to reach a "right answer" as a group.
- Don't try to solve everything—explore the big ideas that will have the most impact.

If you are concerned that the groups won't be comfortable with generating bold options or able to focus enough to get the work done, you may find it helpful to provide them with worksheets that guide them through a series of questions to be answered. Give the groups one-and-a-half to two hours to work. They will feel rushed, but the time limit forces them to generate ideas quickly. If participants in the small groups don't agree, they can present multiple options. We find that the morning session will have primed the creative pump; by the afternoon, the participants are eager to start getting ideas down on paper.

Have the groups focus eighteen to twenty-four months out as a time frame for their design. They are designing an ideal state. By focusing on the future, rather than on practical next steps, the groups are freer to think bigger and not worry so much about the impact of options on the people in the room. Remind them that there will be plenty of time to refine and sequence the change to account for real constraints. At this time they should focus on the ideal toward which the organization should be working. This shifts the focus from merely fixing today's problems to building a new future.

We work in a low-tech manner—flipcharts, markers, sticky notes. Sometimes a group wants to use PowerPoint, but we find that this shifts the focus to presentation mode rather than just capturing ideas in a graphic format. If a group does want to use the computer, reinforce that they should not be using the org chart program and that there are no extra points for making an option look nice at this stage. Ideas are what count.

We suggest that the leader not participate in the option generation work, so as not to influence the discussion. The executive team can be divided among the groups or put into their own working group.

*Sharing and Evaluation.* The last ninety minutes to two hours of the afternoon are spent in sharing and review. Each group presents its work. Other participants ask questions of clarification, but the facilitator ensures that the discussion is nonjudgmental and that alternatives are kept on the table until all the groups have presented. The leader is present, but should be coached to react neutrally to the presentations and only ask clarifying questions. He or she should, however, be sure to express appreciation for the work and effort of the group. The participants, particularly those at lower levels, may be taking political risks with their options and should be reassured that this is a safe forum. Participants will be watching body language and reading between the lines of the leader's comments. Remind the group that no decisions are being made. After all the teams have presented, the facilitator can help summarize the ideas that are similar and the major areas of difference.

The day ends with the leader identifying the topics that will be the focus of the second round of design the next morning. For example, at a charette for a firm shifting from a product-oriented strategy to one with more customer focus, each of the small groups identified the need to create a new post-sale service capability. However, there was not alignment on whether this should be led from the corporate center, managed regionally, or embedded into the business units. Developing more detailed options for this service offering became a topic for the second round of design.

Design thinking benefits from intensive work, sleep, and reflection, and then revisiting and revising. At least one overnight is built into the charette, and sometimes more than one charette is needed. Conclude the first day's work with a relaxing group reception or dinner to encourage networking.

During the evening, the facilitators and the administrative team summarize the day's output and meet with the leader to agree on the topics of focus and groups for the next morning.

### Second Morning: Reviewing, Revising, Detailing

*Review.*    Start the morning by reviewing the first day's output, which should be typed up. This might include a question-and-answer discussion of the strategy, a summary of key themes from the assessment findings discussion, and refinement of the design criteria. Review the common ideas from the options and the areas of disagreement that need to be explored further.

*Detailed Design.*    The bulk of the second morning is spent on another round of design. Be sure to mix groups. Otherwise, a team can get attached to an idea. Small groups working in parallel will become somewhat competitive. This is good: it brings out energy. You don't want the groups to take ownership of any ideas, however. At the end of the charette, the good ideas should be owned by all, with no one remembering who suggested them first.

In the second round, each team will be working on a discrete topic. For example, one group might look at how best to segment the sales force, another at building a service capability, and a third at what new roles are needed in marketing and where they are best placed in the organization. You may want to assign participants to a topic to ensure that the groups are well mixed and that you have the right subject matter expertise in each group. We also find that participants are energized by being able to choose the topic they work on. In this case, put the topics on flipcharts around the room and have participants vote with their feet. You can quickly see if any rebalancing needs to occur in order to ensure robust groups.

This second round can also be used to test the options that are emerging. Select some real scenarios, such as work that is hard to get done today because of friction in the organization, and work that doesn't get done because of capacity, process, or capability gaps. Select some scenarios that reflect work that comes from a variety of sources, such as customer requests and corporate mandates. Look at special projects (for example, acquisitions or plant closings) as well as ongoing work. Have the groups explore how these scenarios would play out in the emerging model.

*Sharing.*   As with the first round of design, give the groups about ninety minutes to work and then have them report out.

### Second Afternoon: Planning and Communication

*Work Streams.*   Following the second round of design, it may be clear that there are some big ideas worth pursuing further, more information to be collected, or specific topics that need focused design attention. If this is the case, ask participants to volunteer to work on developing a charter for each of these work streams—the purpose, deliverable, timeline, and needed internal and external expertise. The groups in the room often become the core teams for these work streams, but the leader may want to reflect after the charette on what framework decisions need to be made, the sequence of activities, and the membership of the work-stream teams before sending anyone off to work.

*Next Steps.*   Depending on the starting point and the progress made, the group may be able to begin sketching out a timeline together, focusing on the sequence of activities. Or, at this stage, the leader may want to summarize the charette accomplishments, express appreciation for the effort and teamwork demonstrated, and lay out the general timeline and sequence in which the work will be carried forward. Although the leader should feel no pressure to make design decisions during the charette, he or she should be quite clear about the overall timeline (generally the next six months) and immediate next steps in the process.

The group may be somewhat disappointed that they don't feel "done" and are leaving with more loose ends and questions then they came with. This is natural and should be acknowledged. The group walks in on the first day, each person wondering what the others are thinking and anxious about the scope of the task before them. By the end of the first afternoon, they are often on a high, feeling great about how much progress they made in just one day. They see a diverse group come together to identify creative and exciting options for the future. By the end of the second day, the focus shifts to implementation. Participants are now overwhelmed, wondering, "How will we get there?" Now that they see where they might be going, the journey seems far and complicated.

The leader can address this reaction by being clear about the process going forward. In addition, if possible, the facilitators might have the group identify some "low-hanging fruit" that can be harvested right away to maintain momentum and send immediate positive signals to the larger organization about the process. These changes should be directly related to the design criteria, but not require structure, metric, or people changes. An example might be that the group suggests forming a team to solve a customer service issue that has languished.

*Communication.*    Before ending the charette, it is important to review what can and cannot be communicated by participants to staff, colleagues, and customers. The rest of the organization will be curious and ask questions about what decisions were made. We suggest that participants do communicate the following:

- Key messages about the strategy and the need for change
- The design criteria
- An overview of the process used (participation, option generation, debate, revision)
- The timeline for next steps

The participants should not share the design options generated. As these are still just possibilities, they could easily create anxiety if discussed out of context.

### Planning and Logistics

*Planning Team.* The planning team is responsible for ensuring that the charette is set up for success. Participants should be able to focus fully on the work without worrying about the mechanics of the meeting. The planning team is usually similar to the core team for the overall project and might include some or all of the following: the leader, HR, OD, strategic planning, project management, communications, and external consultant. The planning team sets the charette agenda, prepares communications and any premeeting activities or reading, determines who will participate, and attends to the logistics of the meeting.

*Facilitators.* The charette requires at least one primary facilitator who is not a participant. The HR business partner should not normally be the facilitator, but rather participate fully in the design work. Use either an external consultant or an internal OD specialist. For a group of more than about twenty, two facilitators are needed. Depending on the complexity of the design task and the likely group dynamics, you may want to have facilitators assist with the small groups. HR colleagues from other business units can serve this role well. Another option is to designate one person from each of the first-round groups as the facilitator for his or her team. Meet with these individuals before the charette to provide them with a template and briefing for helping the small team work together—instructions, timing, and some tips for guiding the discussion.

The role of the lead facilitator is to keep the charette on schedule, provide clear activity instructions, work with the leader or executive team to frame the correct questions and tasks for the iterative work, manage large-group reviews and discussion, and summarize key points and themes. In addition to basic organization design knowledge, facilitating a charette requires a high level of consulting skills and experience in helping diverse groups work through complex problems.

*Administrators.*   An administrative team is necessary to coordinate the materials, audiovisual setup, and breaks and meals, as well as interface with the conference center and support the participants for travel and messages. In addition, they should be prepared to sit in the large-group sessions to capture questions and answers, type up notes, and prepare revisions to the design criteria.

*Logistics.*   The main room for the charette should be set with round tables with seating for six to eight with comfortable swivel chairs. Select a room large enough for small groups to be able to work without disturbing one another and to review material posted on the walls. In addition, arrange for break-out rooms for the major small-group activities. Each table and break-out room should have a flipchart and good markers. In addition, some groups like to work with sticky notes of various sizes as a way to illustrate the various roles and relationships in their design options. Use name tents and tags to facilitate relationship building. Check acoustics and provide a hand-held microphone if sound is a problem.

The charette often becomes the touchstone event in a design process. It ensures that participants understand the complexity of the design decisions. Even if someone doesn't agree with aspects of the final design, he or she will understand that the leader did not have a simple choice to make. Participants leave as advocates of the process and are able to speak authentically about the strategy, the business case for change, and the capabilities needed. They have created new networks and trusting working relationships that will serve as the foundation for further cross-organization collaboration. The leader gains an extended leadership team ready to support implementation and positively influence the change process.

The expense of a charette is not insignificant: participant time away from the job, travel, conference center costs, and facilitation. A leader may question that it is worth the outlay. After guiding and observing many different approaches to organization design projects, we believe that the design charette is a wise investment for both content and process reasons. The range and quality of ideas provided to the leader exceeds any other approach we've seen. In addition, change management and implementation start right at the beginning of the process. The charette accelerates change through the education and understanding that is shared, the working relationships built, and the communication and influence networks established.

## TRANSITION LEADERSHIP

After the charette, the leader will make key framework and staffing decisions and move the organization into the transition phase. Once the executive team is in place, members will be eager to turn their attention away from design and return to the day-to-day work of running the organization. The transition, however, needs strong guidance and project management. This shouldn't be left to the executive team, as it will be a small part of their individual agendas, and responsibility will become diffuse. The core team members will also need to get back to their "day jobs." Although the HR, OD, and strategy leaders will have significant roles in the transition, running the implementation phase may not be the best use of their time. At the same time, the leader should avoid turning this work over to a junior project manager without the clout to push the organization forward.

For a significant change, the leader should consider the appointment of a "transition manager." While the leader and executive team remain accountable for the quality of the transition, the transition manager takes on day-to-day responsibility for execution. The transition manager is responsible for the implementation plan, including the following elements:

- Managing the project plan (tasks, milestones, owner, timeline, status, dependencies)
- Ensuring that all the implementation work-stream teams are moving forward
- Identifying what new teams, relationships, and networks need to be built and ensuring that the right people are meeting
- Ensuring that the executive team agenda focuses on the right topics and that the members are being held accountable for the behaviors that support the new organizational model
- Managing communications, feedback, and engagement activities
- Tracking performance, measuring success, and proactively suggesting adjustments to the executive team

The transition manager is best staffed by a high-credibility, high-potential line manager who is temporarily elevated to the executive team, or a well-respected executive heading for retirement. He or she should be a strong project manager who understands organization as a lever of strategy and has strong influence bases and skills. If the change is on a large scale, this can be a full-time role for some limited time, typically six to twelve months.

## MEASURING SUCCESS

An organization design project presents so many variables in a unique context that it can be difficult to measure success. Here is a dashboard that we use for ourselves, which may be useful to you as well.

### Business Outcomes

Financial and customer results are the ultimate business outcomes. However, even when you can draw a cause-and-effect relationship between organization design decisions and business results, they are lagging indicators. It is too late to change course once you find out that the business isn't doing well.

In contrast, the capabilities you identify to be your design criteria make excellent leading indicators; they can be measured, and adjustments can be made midcourse. Leading indicators are the assumptions that "if we do $x$, then $y$ will occur." For example, "If we improve our innovation process from concept to design, we will get products to market quicker. Reducing new product development cycle time will give us an advantage over our competitors in developing markets." The innovation process capability can then be translated into a series of concrete measures that are tracked.

### Client Satisfaction

The next measure is whether the leader and executive team (the clients) agree that using a disciplined organization design process allowed them to make better decisions and work more efficiently. Do the clients feel that the organization design process, tools, and facilitation resulted in better decisions than the clients could have reached by themselves? Did they get to the end result faster?

### Project Discipline

For the core team, the quality of project management is also an important measure. Ask, "How well have we met milestones and commitments? Did we get the work done on time and on budget to the specs we set out? If we were a consulting firm, would our clients feel that they had gotten good value and that we were easy to do business with?"

### Internal Working Relationships

This measure applies to the HR team specifically. In many companies, a centralized OD resource works with or through HR generalists or other internal support groups. Any friction and confusion shows to the client. Ask, "How well did we work together?"

### Learning

Finally, we believe that every organization design project is a learning experience for leadership, employees, and the HR team. When learning is a measure of success, you ensure that the experience doesn't build just individual skills but an organizational capability. You might ask, "What did we do well? What can we do better?" but also, "How well have we documented and shared what we have learned?" This might take the form of postmortems, debriefings, lunch-and-learns, contributions to the intranet site, and additions to the organization design toolkit.

# Learning to Lead Organization Design

I F YOU ARE READING THIS AS A BUSINESS LEADER, we encourage you to view organization design as an essential element of your personal effectiveness as a leader.

Beginning in the 1950s, Peter Drucker began building on the much earlier, foundational work of Henry Fayol and Frederick Taylor. He brought a behavioral perspective to the art and science of management. He defined the impact that leadership had on performance. The study of leadership has progressed as a major field, and from Fred Herzberg, David McClelland, and Warren Bennis to Daniel Goleman we have learned how leaders unleash the power of motivated, effective talent, inspired by great vision.

Over time, however, theories of leadership have become increasingly narrow in focus, built around prescriptive frameworks. This is in contrast to Drucker's expansive and highly integrated picture of business enterprise management, within which leadership is a necessary, but not sufficient, element.

## The Intersection of Talent and Organization

Efforts to distinguish leadership from the seemingly mundane tasks of management have been useful in crystallizing the power of vision, courage, and emotional intelligence to drive extraordinary effort. But leadership studies that focus on great teams—from sports to heroic product development labs— tell only a partial story. There is little point in setting a compelling vision and building a motivated workforce without the hard work of developing the organizational capabilities to activate them.

We recently completed a coaching assignment with an executive we will call John, a high-potential division general manager who had been given charge of a fast-growth, billion-dollar unit of a larger company two years before we met him. John's boss had expected great things from him based on his creativity, passion, and terrific people skills, combined with his seventeen years of experience in the industry, mostly as a very successful sales leader. He had delivered year-over-year, top-line growth of 15 percent or more for the previous five years. He came into the role specifically to expand the division's success formula into new markets. John's business strategies were guided by his terrific instincts about his global customers. And he inspired his extended leadership team with his vision and the challenge they had been presented. But as general manager, John struggled to deliver on the expected growth goals during his first two years at the helm.

A deep dive into the dynamics of the organization revealed that despite the great affection his team felt for him, many had become frustrated with what amounted to John's inability to transition the business from a highly entrepreneurial division, mostly doing business in North America and parts of Europe, into a scaled, multinational company that was actually expected to lead the rest of the corporation into new and more complex markets.

It was clear that John had learned very little about how to scale his leadership impact by creating such organizational capabilities as launching global products, managing strategic partners, or establishing infrastructure and talent in China and India. Like many general managers who struggle with this transition from functional management to business management, John assumed that when he articulated his expectations, good people would bring his ideas to life. In a sense, he overestimated his own powers of persuasion and oversimplified the importance of an aligned organization for executing a complex strategy.

The difference between executives who lead great teams of people and those who lead powerful organizations is leverage, integration, and repeatability of results—all achieved through capability building. One definition of capability is that when the great man is gone, the great organization survives. Even the erratic, eccentric, and brilliant Steve Jobs learned this with the help of his foil and managerial counterpoint, Tim Cook, Apple's highly disciplined and process-oriented COO. When A. G. Lafley stepped down in 2009 as CEO of P&G, what he left behind was an organization that was much more capable of competing in global consumer markets than the one he inherited. Lafley led a painful journey at P&G to implement a global organization model begun by a predecessor. He managed with courage through a risky, complex transition that took years. Lafley is a study in methodical, thoughtful building of organizational capability more than one in charismatic, visionary leadership.

The pace of change and the uncertainty in today's business challenges demand more agility from organizations. As market situations change, organization and leadership should not remain static; but new research argues that rather than merely reacting to situational change, companies that outperform their peers are more proactive about evolving leadership and organization (Corporate Leadership Council, 2010). As an example, across-the-board downsizing is replaced with deliberate repurposing of resources and asymmetrical investments in talent, depending on where the future growth is.

Jack Welch understood the importance of getting his leaders to think about organization as well as talent when he retooled the talent and organization review process in his early years at GE. Unilever and others have adopted similar integrated, annual leadership and organization effectiveness reviews in recent years. In these organization reviews, leaders are challenged to think through a series of questions intended to focus them on organizational capability and capacity needs in the future. Given the growth choices that have been made, what work needs top management attention? How will we establish presence in emerging markets in the coming years? What functions will have the most impact on growth in the future? Can you afford the organization you have? What positions in the organization are the key learning grounds for high-potential leaders? Marriott goes a step further by assessing capabilities as part of its annual talent review process, and it has internal organization design experts on hand to help respond to issues.

Questions like those in GE's review frame the typical leadership and talent discussions in a new light. The question of how and where to use the specific talents and experiences of a given executive is far more interesting in the context of a longer-term—horizon 2 or horizon 3—view of the organization changes that may lie ahead (Baghai, Coley, and White, 1999). Welch saw this as an integrated dialogue and expected his executives to do the same. Executives at GE, such as Larry Bossidy, became instinctive about creating the right combinations of organization and executive talent in operating divisions as a means of driving execution of business unit strategy at GE and later at Allied-Signal and Honeywell (Bossidy, Charan, and Burck, 2002).

## Building General Managers' Organization Know-How

Organization design is not a once-and-done or occasional event. Rather it is an ongoing component of good management process. Executives at the enterprise level and in major operating units and functions should become skilled at using the frameworks spelled out in this book and others like them. We believe this know-how is core to the work of leaders today and can be thought of as three sets of skills:

**Design**
- Define capabilities necessary to execute strategic goals
- Surface and resolve organizational and talent barriers to execution
- Act as an architect to align business processes, structure, roles, and reward systems in order to drive new results

**Activate**
- Invest in talent where pivotal work takes place
- Manage the flow of leadership talent across the business
- Teach other senior executives their roles and decision rights
- Help managers who work for you to build capable organizations under them

**Govern**
- Use the four governance levers to balance power relationships in the matrix; welcome conflict, put it on the table, and use diverse views to benefit the business
- Manage the top team to be certain that objectives are aligned vertically and horizontally across the organization

How do managers learn these skills? They begin by becoming aware. Frameworks such as the ones in this book can be used as tools for learning and guidance. Finding an internal or external organization effectiveness partner is also a good idea, even if you're learning together.

### Learn by Doing

Experience is still the best source of senior leadership development. Some have argued that perhaps 70 percent of senior leadership development comes from experience, 20 percent comes from coaching, and just 10 percent comes from classroom instruction (Lombardo and Eichinger, 1989).

Implementing a new organization design inside the corporation is one way to provide a "managed experience" to accelerate the growth of high-potential general management candidates. The challenges of leading change through complex organization transitions provide exceptional leadership development opportunities. There are at least two ways to gain leadership development experience in organization design: by participating in design decisions and by leading the transition to a new design.

*Learn by Making Design Decisions.*    The work of redesigning an organization presents a special opportunity to grow leaders. High-potential managers can be selected to participate on the design teams to work through strategy and execution issues and determine the best way to align structure, process, roles, and decision rights around a given strategic challenge or opportunity. In the design process, members learn to see the relationships between structure, process, metrics, and talent, and they learn the organizational frameworks and models that are useful as they take on larger leadership roles. GE, P&G, and many others have used organization design teams skillfully in this manner.

During the last few years at Nike, high-potential leaders on design teams have learned to analyze the benefits and risks of organization design options. Nike communicated widely its transition to consumer categories as a key organization focus. More than one hundred key leaders worked through the details of a new category-based structure, new process designs, and new role definitions and decision rights, and have participated in design and organization development thinking over a two-year period. Organization development experts, both internal and external, supported the design teams, shared many of the tools and practices featured in this book, and taught leaders how to apply them.

New general managers were able to understand and influence all the elements of organization that influenced the kind of consumer experience they sought to create.

*Learn by Leading Major Change in Organization Design.* Leading major change through the implementation of a new organization design is another powerful development experience. Especially if the new organization design produces resistance due its countercultural nature, leaders who assume new roles in these new structures are tested in unusual ways and will grow through successes and failures alike. The learning is very much enhanced by the fact that these change leaders will be held accountable for the outcomes of their action-learning projects.

Typically there are high degrees of ambiguity during these transitions. It is quite useful to see how leaders respond to ill-defined change problems and to coach them through those problems as part of their learning. Opportunities for learning include defining the interests of various stakeholders in the change process, anticipating points of resistance, and planning to overcome them, especially if there is a requirement to manage "virtual" business units that will rely heavily on matrixed ownership across cultures, geographic units, functions, and market conditions. Strong HR partners support emerging leaders and help them learn how to use staff people effectively in complex leadership challenges.

Returning to the Nike example, high-potential VP candidates were placed in new category-based business units, and each worked through the complexities of how to finish the detailed design work for their category, staff the key jobs, launch the new cross-functional team, and partner with a highly complex set of stakeholders to align roles and expectations across functions and geographic units.

### Provide Support During the Development Experience

Some of the best executive development opportunities occur under pressure. As organizations are reconfigured, companies can provide leaders with exceptional learning experiences—as well as challenging tests of leadership skills—by asking them to lead transitions from existing structures and processes to substantially new ones. Engineering these transitions to maximize learning means creating a framework for change leaders to follow and providing support and coaching through the change process. And it means assessing leaders to find those who thrive in the uncertainty of major change. The rewards of this conscious, planned approach to change are significant for the growth of leaders.

Here are some suggestions for successfully using design projects to develop leaders:

1. *Select* candidates to participate in the design process and to lead the change who are
   - High-potential managers who are likely to succeed but need to be tested and stretched out of their comfort zone
   - Strategic and business-oriented people who can contribute innovative thinking to the design process related to their piece of the organization
   - Objective team members, able to be completely open to the best design options for the business and unbiased by personal ambitions

2. *Educate* managers throughout the design, building, and transition process:
   - Teach them to use organization design tools and methods as they need them to complete the task
   - Provide internal or external organization development assistance

3. *Sponsor* the change process with more senior executives to whom the leaders can turn in order to
   - Remove major barriers, and support the larger change process
   - Delegate real responsibility to leaders of new units—including allowing measured failure
   - Provide nonevaluative mentoring and coaching

4. *Assess* performance and provide feedback on a regular basis by observing performance under challenging new circumstances. Use a set of clear criteria that measures how well the emerging executives lead change and how well they

learn the capability-building tools—as well as how well they manage complex projects.

We began this book by arguing that leaders can directly drive results only through three levers: setting the right strategy, picking the right talent, and building an effective organization. The challenges that business leaders face in today's global, wired, and matrixed world are both exciting and daunting. Future senior leaders cannot rely exclusively on experts in strategy, talent, and organization but must build personal competency and confidence in these domains. Success will be measured in terms of the expansive and integrated thinking and leadership behaviors that can work those levers together to produce superior results for the many demanding stakeholders that business will serve in this new century.

# References

Arons, R. M., and Ruh, R. *American Hospital Supply Corp.: An Historic Incubator of Leadership Talent*. Los Angeles: Korn-Ferry, 2004.

Axelrod, R. H. *Terms of Engagement: Changing the Way We Change Organizations*. San Francisco: Berrett-Koehler, 2002.

Baghai, M., Coley, S., and White, D. *The Alchemy of Growth: Practical Insights for Building the Enduring Enterprise*. London: Orion Business Books, 1999.

Bain & Co. "World Class Retail Capabilities Benchmarking." Boston: Bain & Co., 2008.

Bartlett, C., and Ghoshal, S. *Managing Across Borders: The Transnational Solution*. Boston: Harvard Business School Press, 1989.

Bossidy, L., Charan, R., and Burck, C. *Execution: The Discipline of Getting Things Done*. New York: Crown Business, 2002.

Boudreau, J., and Ramstad, P. M. *Beyond HR: The New Science of Human Capital*. Boston: Harvard Business School Press, 2007.

Brown, T. *Change by Design: How Design Thinking Transforms Organizations and Inspires Innovation*. New York: Harper Business, 2009.

Bulkeley, W. M. "Spinning a Global Plan." *Wall Street Journal*, Feb. 14, 2008, p. 1.

Charan, R., Drotter, S., and Noel, J. *The Leadership Pipeline: How to Build the Leadership Powered Company*. San Francisco: Jossey-Bass, 2001.

Corporate Leadership Council. "Developmental Experiences." Arlington, Va.: Corporate Executive Board, 2003.

Corporate Leadership Council. "Managing Leadership Performance Risks." Arlington, Va.: Corporate Executive Board, 2010.

DeGraff, J., and Quinn, S. E. *Leading Innovation: How to Jump Start Your Company's Growth Engine.* New York: McGraw-Hill, 2007.

Drucker, P. F. *Management: Tasks, Responsibilities, Practices.* New York: Harper & Row, 1973.

Galbraith, J. R. *Designing Organizations: An Executive Briefing on Strategy, Structure and Process.* San Francisco: Jossey-Bass, 1995.

Galbraith, J. R. *Designing Matrix Organizations That Actually Work.* San Francisco: Jossey-Bass, 2009.

Govindarajan, V., and Trimble, C. *Ten Rules for Strategic Innovators: From Idea to Execution.* Boston: Harvard Business School Press, 2005.

Heywood, S., Spungin, J., and Turnbull, D. "Cracking the Complexity Code." *McKinsey Quarterly,* May 2007, pp. 85–95.

Holstein, W. J. "Little Companies, Big Export." *Business Week,* Apr. 13, 1992, pp. 70–72.

Jaques, E. *Requisite Organization: A Total System for Effective Managerial Organization and Managerial Leadership for the 21st Century: Amended.* Arlington, Va.: Cason Hall, 1989.

Jaruzelski, B., Dehoff, K., and Bordia, R. "Money Isn't Everything." *Strategy + Business,* Winter 2005, http://www.insme.org/documenti/ MoneyIsnt.pdf.

Kates, A. "Organization Design." In W. Rothwell, J. M. Stavros, R. L. Sullivan, and A. Sullivan (eds.), *Practicing Organization Development: A Guide for Leading Change.* (3rd. ed.) San Francisco: Pfeiffer, 2010.

Kates, A., and Galbraith, J. R. *Designing Your Organization: Using the Star Model to Solve Five Critical Design Challenges.* San Francisco: Jossey-Bass, 2007.

Kesler, G. "Why the Leadership Bench Never Gets Deeper: Ten Insights About Executive Talent Development." *People & Strategy,* 2002, *25*(1), 32–44. http://www.chrs.net/images/chrs_papers/ teninsights.pdf.

Kesler, G., and Kirincic, P. "Roadmaps for Developing General Managers: The Experience of a Healthcare Giant." *Journal of the Human Resource Planning Society, Human Resources Planning,* 2005, *28*(3), 24–37.

Kesler, G., and Schuster, M. "New Thinking from Drucker's Legacy: Design Your Governance Model to Make the Matrix Work." *People & Strategy,* 2009, *32*(4), 16–25.

Kim, W. C., and Mauborgne, R. *Blue Ocean Strategy.* Boston: Harvard Business School Press, 2005.

Lombardo, M. M., and Eichinger, R. W. "Eighty-Eight Assignments for Development in Place." Greensboro, N.C.: Center for Creative Leadership, June 1989.

Lucio, A. "Global Brand Management in the Pepsi Generation." *Leading Global Brands Bulletin.* Global Marketing Effectiveness blog, April 25, 2008. http://globalmarketingeffectiveness.blogspot .com/2008/05/global-brand-management-in-pepsi.html.

Mahler, W. R. *Structure, Power, and Results: How to Organize Your Company for Optimum Performance.* Midland Park, N.J.: Mahler, 1975.

Mahler, W. R., and Drotter, S. J. *Succession Planning Handbook for the Chief Executive.* Midland Park, N.J.: Mahler, 1986.

"Making the Emotional Case for Change: An Interview with Chip Heath." *McKinsey Quarterly,* Mar. 2010. http://www.mckinsey quarterly.com/Making_the_emotional_case_for_change_An_ interview_with_Chip_Heath_2543.

Martin, R. *The Design of Business: Why Design Thinking Is the Next Competitive Advantage.* Boston: Harvard Business School Press, 2009.

McGirt, E. "Revolution in San Jose: A Hard-Core Republican Turns Cisco into a Socialist Enterprise." *Fast Company,* Jan. 2009, pp. 88–134.

Moore, G. A. *Dealing with Darwin: How Great Companies Innovate at Every Phase of Their Evolution.* New York: Penguin Group, 2005.

Morrison, C. "How to Innovate Like Apple." bnet (CBS Business Network), 2009. http://www.bnet.com/2403-13501_23-330240 .html.

Nadler, D. A., Spencer, J. L. and the Delta Consulting Group. *Executive Teams*. San Francisco: Jossey-Bass, 1998.

Osterwalder, A., and Pigneur, Y. *Business Model Generation: A Handbook for Visionaries, Game Changers, and Challengers*. Amsterdam: Osterwalder and Pigneur, 2009.

Rogers, P., and Blenko, M. "Who Has the D? How Clear Decision Roles Enhance Organizational Performance." *Harvard Business Review*, 2006, *84*(1), 52–59.

Schein, E. H. *Organizational Culture and Leadership*. San Francisco: Jossey-Bass, 2004.

Simons, R. *Levers of Control: How Managers Use Innovative Control Systems to Drive Strategic Renewal*. Boston: Harvard Business School Press, 1995.

Simons, R. *Levers of Organization Design: How Managers Use Accountability Systems for Greater Performance and Commitment*. Boston: Harvard Business School Press, 2005.

Snyder, N. T., and Duarte, D. L. *Unleashing Innovation: How Whirlpool Transformed an Industry*. San Francisco: Jossey-Bass, 2008.

Sonne, P. "Power Tweaks Power Reckitt." *Wall Street Journal*, Feb. 11, 2010, p. B8.

Sull, D. "Competing Through Organizational Agility." *McKinsey Quarterly*, Dec. 2009. http://www.mckinseyquarterly.com/Competing_through_organizational_agility_2488.

# About the Authors

**Gregory Kesler** consults with corporations in organization design, executive talent management, and human resource planning. He has led whole-company redesign projects and has developed and implemented succession planning practices and executive assessment at many global companies.

Greg is the author of numerous articles and book chapters, including "New Thinking from Drucker's Legacy: Design Your Governance Model to Make the Matrix Work" (*People & Strategy*, Winter 2010) and "Using a Reorganization to Test and Grow High-Potential Leaders" (in *Leadership Development*, Pfeiffer, 2009). His article on HR transformation received the Walker Prize from HR People & Strategy. Greg is also an editor of the journal *People & Strategy*.

Before beginning his consulting career, Greg held senior HR management positions in the United States and Europe for three Fortune 200 companies. At Pitney Bowes, he served as vice president of human resources for North America. Greg lives in Wilton, Connecticut, with his family.

**Amy Kates** works with leaders and their teams to assess organizational issues, reshape structures and processes, and build depth of management capability. In addition to her consulting work, she teaches organization design in the Executive MBA program at the Executive School of Business in Denmark and through Cornell University. Amy is also an editor of the journal *People & Strategy*.

Amy is a coauthor, with Jay Galbraith, of the book *Designing Your Organization: Using the Star Model to Solve Five Critical Design Challenges* (Jossey-Bass, 2007) and, with Jay Galbraith and Diane Downey, of the book *Designing Dynamic Organizations: A Hands-On Guide for Leaders at All Levels* (Amacom, 2002). She has published numerous articles and book chapters on the topics of organization design and talent management, including "The Challenges of General Manager Transitions" (in *Filling the Management Pipeline*, Center for Creative Leadership, 2005) and "Matrix Structures and Virtual Collaboration" (in *The Handbook of High-Performance Virtual Teams*, Jossey-Bass, 2008).

Her article "(Re)Designing the HR Organization" was awarded the 2007 Walker Prize by HR People & Strategy. Her ideas on emerging models for human resources have been used by leading companies around the world as the basis for the design of their HR functions. Amy lives in New York City with her family.

# Index